FOR **MEN** ONLY
How To Survive Marriage

FOR **MEN** ONLY

How To Survive Marriage

By

EVAN KELIHER

Illustrated by **BOB McMAHON**

CCC PUBLICATIONS • LOS ANGELES

Published by

CCC Publications
20306 Tau Place
Chatsworth, CA 91311

Manufactured in the United States of America

Cover design © 1990 CCC Publications

Illustrations © 1990 Evan Keliher

Cover & interior art by Bob McMahon

Cover Production by The Creative Place

ISBN: 0-918259-30-4

Pre-publication Edition — 1/91
First Printing — 7/91.

Contents

INTRODUCTION

Okay, why such a book? Do men really need a guide to marriage? Is such a thing even possible? Is it sexist? Why not a guide for women — or couples? And who the hell am I to think I know enough about the subject to write a book on it?

Well, *somebody* out there needs help. They say half of all marriages today will end in divorce, and it's at least implied a lot of the rest aren't doing all that well, either. There's no center anymore — whatever the hell that means. No rules. How are guys supposed to know which end is up if somebody doesn't tell them what's going on?

Of course men need a guide to marriage, and they always have. Poor Socrates was saddled with Xanthippe, the model for a shrewish woman. Juvenal must have needed help with his mother-in-law because he wrote in the 1st century A.D., "While your wife's mother lives, expect no peace."

George Bernard Shaw said, "You think you are (the woman's) suitor; that you are the pursuer and she the pursued; that it is your part to woo, to persuade, to prevail, to overcome. Fool: it is you who are pursued, the marked down quarry, the destined prey."

Guys don't know this. They have no idea that the sloe-eyed creature with the breathless boobs and long, nylon-clad legs also has a mind that's far

1

superior to their own in cunning and deviousness. They inhale a bunch of pheromones and zero in on their targets with a kind of primeval radar and women draw them in like a sideshow barker drawing farmers to the bearded lady's tent.

Do men need a book on how to survive marriage? Obviously. Isn't it only fair that they have at least one book to counter the hundreds available to their adversaries in our nation's bookstores? Shouldn't they be warned of the perils, advised of strategies, notified of their rights (in those states that allow men to have rights, that is)? In other words, don't men need a level playing field in the marriage game?

As for my credentials, well, few know more about marriage than I do, at least insofar as practical experience is concerned. I've been married forever and have learned many valuable lessons along the way. If I'm not an expert on the subject, no one is.

So I thought I'd do a useful service for MANkind and write down a few observations garnered from my own experiences with holy matrimony in the hope that I might save some innocent sap from making similar mistakes and sharing the fate of most husbands who end up pitiful, broken creatures without spines or even personalities they can call their own.

Disgraceful.

One

WHY WE DO IT

Just about everybody gets married eventually, and lots of 'em more than once. It can't be helped. Why? Because there are immutable forces at work busily roping us in from the onset of puberty all the way to senility and beyond, that's why. It all has to do with pheromones, those mysterious, air-borne chemicals that inflame men's minds, and nature's law and fate and DNA and astrology and long, slim, nylon-clad legs and cleavage and sensual eyes and perfume and ecstasy real or imagined and...

See what I mean? The whole business is entirely beyond our control. One minute we belong to gangs and build tree houses and collect baseball cards, and the next thing we know girls show up and we're goners. Bam! Just like that. It's all over. Wedding bells and rings — in our noses, usually — bring in-laws and mortgages and choices narrowed from unlimited to none, and all because a lot of pheromones get loose.

What's worse, right from the start men and women are working at cross purposes. Most girls hit thirteen and they immediately start laying in hope chests and reordering people's lives while boys at that age are laying plans to get laid. Girls instinctively build imaginary nests while boys dream of adventure in foreign lands — with heroic roles for themselves, of course. Boys ride off into assorted sunsets and girls are left behind with broken hearts. Boys slay dragons; girls get rescued. That's how guys see it, but girls have a somewhat different slant on things and a determination to convert us to it come what may.

All the time we're dreaming these dreams, the girls are busily arranging things so we end up as accountants instead of pirates. They have their own agendum and entrapping some unwary sap into matrimony is high on the list of priorities. It's not even a conscious thought; it comes to 'em naturally along with the first blast of pheromones. One day they look around at their male classmates and say, "How can I trick one of these jokers into a lifetime commitment to do my bidding and provide luxuries for me and mine?" They begin laying plans at once to bring about this utopia.

So we start off with a conflict. Guys envision life unfolding in a particular way and girls see something entirely different. We can't be both pirates and accountants, though it's possible to combine pirating with some professions. Law and politics come to mind, for instance. No, it's a lost cause from the start; boys will not be pirates if girls have anything to say about the matter.

Well, how do they go about distracting us from lives on the bounding main? Easy. They do it with those pheromones. And a thousand tricks passed from mother to daughter since the first little chippy daubed some berry juice on her lips and paralyzed every male in the village. In other words, they do it with sex, or, more often, mere promises of sex, for if you just *promise* the average guy sex his mind fogs up, his judgment vanishes, and he signs up for accounting courses.

Of course, most girls don't care all that much about sex themselves, you know. It's just the main arrow in their feminine quiver, their chief strategy, as it were. They know we're powerless where sex is concerned, that man's libido governs all his actions, and they have said libidos right where they want 'em. What's more, the cleverest ones manage to make us think the whole thing is *our* idea and they're just acceding to our wishes. We're even made to feel obligated as a result of their largess and agree to sign on for a lifetime cruise paid for with our credit cards.

Unbelievable.

As I said, it starts with puberty and pheromones and leads inevitably to matrimony — holy or otherwise. Since there's almost nothing we can do about it, it behooves us to study the thing closely in order to limit final damages as much as possible. It's true that prevention is wiser than cure, and never more so than when signing yourself into a lifetime deal with a beclouded mind and warped sense of judgment.

SURVIVAL RULES:

1. **Women are schemers who unhesitatingly employ chemical warfare, i.e., pheromones, to entrap us.**
2. **Men are governed by their libidos and thereby rendered helpless by these pheromones.**
3. **No man can escape them, so we must learn to defend ourselves in an unequal struggle.**

Two

HOW IT ALL STARTS

As I said earlier, it's those damn pheromones. Girls get 'em at puberty and it's all downhill for us from there on.

Take, say, a seventh or eighth grade class anywhere. You're twelve or thirteen, it's a lazy spring day with bright sunlight splashed all over the room and the teacher's mumbling some nonsense about fractions or verbs or whatever. You're idly bouncing paperwads off the nape of Nellie Aames' neck four rows away when all of a sudden there's this little explosion deep inside your brain somewhere.

You look around to see what the hell's going on and your eye lights on little Emma Tuttle, but it's not the same Emma Tuttle you've known since kindergarten. She's changed somehow. You can't put your finger on it, but there's an air about her you never noticed before.

It's the pheromones, of course. The things have suddenly burst out of Emma and floated free in the ambient air and jolted into your teen-age brain and zapped your reasoning center for all time. From now on your life will be influenced by pheromones, your very thoughts modified by 'em. Nature has thrown you a curve ball and it's a beauty.

So now you're aware of girls. You lose interest in a lot of boy stuff that once fascinated you. Right away you quit the clubhouse with the stringent "no girls allowed" rule and deep-six your GI Joe collection in favor of a comb and brush set and mirror.

You dress differently, bathe more often, assume phony postures and begin laying plans to score with little Emma. It's true you aren't exactly sure what scoring entails, but you know it's something you want to do, and the sooner the better.

Emma, meanwhile, has no such plans herself since girls don't score but rather get scored upon and they know this instinctively at a very early age. In fact, Emma will direct all her attention for the next several years to prevent any scoring from taking place anywhere in her vicinity.

It used to be that the Emmas of the world would persist in withholding it until they had some poor clown all tied up in legal documents and sworn oaths before they'd give it up, but that's been modified somewhat today. Most girls nowadays have surrendered all at sixteen or so, but this fact has had little effect on the rules in the war between the sexes.

Anyway, you spend your high school years surrounded by these pheromone fountains and live in a cauldron of confusion and anxiety and insecurity while your libido is driven wild by air-borne chemicals. You're at the mercy of any mere slip of a girl who shows a little cleavage or reveals eight or nine inches of tantalizing thigh or even just looks at you and smiles ever so slightly.

You're vulnerable and the girls know it. If they aren't sharp enough to pick it up themselves, their mothers tell 'em. As fathers show boys how to bat and shoot baskets, so mothers teach daughters coquetry and subterfuge. By the time the pheromones fly, the average girl is well-schooled in the arts of deception, dalliance, and double-dealing.

In olden times, about thirty or so years ago, a lot of girls had nailed a husband within months of leaving high school, and they did it in the classic, time-honored way, too. They got knocked up. It was easy. By graduation the boys were reduced to sexual automatons, mere robots run by their own hormones. The girls had cagily held out on 'em all this time, of course, and when they finally gave in the average sex-mad eighteen-year-old guy was easy prey.

A carefully chosen moment, a romantic setting (the back seat of a Chevy would do), and she allowed herself to be overpowered and gave him some. Naturally, she created the impression that she was reluctant in the extreme and only gave in at last because she loved the poor sap. It's crucial that he believed this so that when she turned up pregnant later it'd be all his fault and he had to assume responsibility for his acts. That is, he had to marry the little conniver.

That's why the average age for marriage was six or seven years earlier than it is today. Birth control was less than an exact science then and to fool around at all almost surely led to marriage and early parenthood. Today's kids are lucky. No one needs to get pregnant if she doesn't want to, nor does she have to stay pregnant unless she elects to do so. Only a true half-wit would fall for the old "I'm-pregnant-you-have-to-marry-me" dodge today and girls are therefore unable to snare a husband via this scheme.

Still, guys are so vulnerable to those ubiquitous pheromones that they're knocked off in wholesale lots without actual entrapment. It's enough that girls are everywhere working their magic and way-laying the unwary with their usual complement of low-cut blouses, nylon-clad legs, subtle perfumes, uplift bras, and assorted paints, creams, lipsticks and what have you. It's a wonder *any* guys retain their bachelorhood past their twenty-first birthday.

Even so, most of 'em eventually succumb and find themselves playing a leading role in a legal ceremony that will forever change their lives in undreamed of ways.

They become husbands and that's an experience nothing in life has prepared 'em for. Still, even if it's new to newly married guys, the institution of marriage itself has been around forever and countless millions of other guys have lived through it and they've found out certain things along the way. It's a fact man's marital problems haven't changed since ancient times; the answers are there, you only have to find them.

Remember, not to know history is to repeat it.

SURVIVAL RULES:
1. **Most women are instinctive hussies.**
2. **Women hold all the aces.**
3. **Don't fall for the old "I'm knocked up" routine.**
4. **Learn from history and save yourself a lot of trouble.**

Three

EARLY DANGER SIGNS

Okay, so let's suppose you're a young guy who's managed to reach his mid-twenties and is still single. Then one day you meet a woman and decide, erroneously, as a rule, that she's in some way special and different from the rest and you find yourself getting serious and even considering marriage sooner or later. It'll be sooner if she has her way, of course, but that's a given.

Now, then, what are some things you should look out for? Are there signs that will tip you off as to what the future may hold with this woman? Of course there are, and the wise man will check 'em out before he gets in over his head.

For example, know that one day she'll end up looking like — and almost certainly *be* like — her mother. Oh, I can hear the cries of outrage from all the women out there denying that this is so, but it is and you can count on it. While there are exceptions, they're damn few.

If her old lady is a three hundred pounder, you'd damn well better like fat women. If her mother's house is ill-kept, so will her daughter's be. If her mother has had four husbands, yours will likely be a short marriage. If her mother is a world-class nag, you'll find yourself living with a world-class nag when you marry the daughter. All the signs are there to be read if only you'll pay attention.

10

"HOW DARE YOU SAY I'M JUST LIKE MY MOTHER!"

11

Well, how soon should a guy adopt a wary attitude and start looking for danger signs?

On the first date, that's when. Size this dame up. Keep an eye out for aberrations, measure the cut of her jib, try to see how her mind works — if she's got one. Can she speak English? Can you detect an odd glint in her eye? Are there scars behind her ears indicating four or five face-lifts? Does she talk a lot about her mother, former husband(s), biological clock, interest in the occult, the Second Coming? All are ominous signs that all's not well.

You should probe skillfully to find out her true nature. For example, suppose you're a real sports nut, the kind of guy who loves football on TV and covets his season tickets for the local hockey team. Naturally, the wily creature will feign an interest in these things too in an effort to win you over and get your ass properly bound up in legal entanglements and lifelong commitments, and it's up to you to see through this deception before it's too late.

Watch for little revealing signs. Does she spend half the game in the john or at the refreshment stand? Does she cheer at inappropriate times? Does she know one sport from another? Or one player from another? Does she watch games on TV when you're not there? A few pointed questions will let you know.

For example, suppose there's a big playoff game on TV on Sunday and you're going with some buddies. The next time you see her ask her if she watched the game. A real fan wouldn't miss it but a pretender would. Unless she can recap the whole thing in detail, you'll know she didn't watch it and therefore isn't really interested in football at all — or any other sport, either.

This means once you marry her she'll drop all pretence and come out foursquare against sports in all forms and nag the hell out of you every time you switch on a football game or try to sneak off with your pals for a softball game somewhere.

Check her out *before* you marry her, not after.

The truth is, the so-called romantic marriage where two people depend on "love" to guide 'em is a pretty bankrupt idea. Look around. The marital shambles you see everywhere is what you get when everybody marries for so-called love. Love only lasts a week or two and then you're stuck with whatever's left.

Perhaps old-fashioned arranged marriages were better, the kind where parents got together and negotiated a deal everyone could live with. The couple was matched in terms of education, social standing, religion, and politics. The girl's folks handed over a predetermined number of pigs or bars of silver or whatever, and it was a done deal.

And who cared if they weren't desperately in love? What the hell happened to the "love" in all the busted marriages we see out there? Let's face it, romantic love is a very ephemeral thing, so ephemeral, in fact, that it often can't even be found a fortnight after the honeymoon ends.

No, you've got to watch this romantic love business. A guy can get in real trouble going this route.

SURVIVAL RULES:

1. Women are basically all alike — the apparent differences are illusory.
2. Most women are replicas of their mothers, so check out her old lady.
3. Suspect her motives from the first date and look for signs of deception.
4. Beware of so-called romantic marriages — it's more important to know her credit rating and work history.

Four

THE PRENUPTIAL AGREEMENT

If you have any possessions you want to keep like, say, a car or a stereo or a collection of erotica from Siam, you need a prenuptial agreement. They're all the vogue these days and for a damn good reason. The world is full of scheming women who'd like nothing better than to trick you into marriage and then skin your ass in the divorce to follow. A wise man covers said ass with a prenuptial agreement.

Of course, if you've got real assets like a thriving business or an inherited fortune, it's *imperative* you get one. I've seen whole empires swallowed up by some grasping female where the poor sap didn't think to protect himself beforehand. Don't let that happen to you.

Get a lawyer, a good one. F. Lee Bailey if you can find him, or at least one experienced in dealing with the most cunning and duplicitous creatures on Earth, i.e., women. Be sure the contract's chock full of obfuscating flyspecks and written in legalese Judge Learned Hand wouldn't be able to decipher. Include lots of ersatz Latin. And plaster it all over with an assortment of vari-colored ribbons and seals and stamps to lend it an air of authenticity so when you go to court later it'll impress the judge.

Don't let your betrothed have a lawyer of her own if you can help it. Use her sex's own arguments against her to pull this off. When a guy asks for a prenuptial agreement the woman is pissed-off because she sees her future threatened and her own rights diminished. She usually counters by pouting and feigning anger and declaring that if he really loved her he'd trust her and marry her as is.

Okay, so hoist her on her own petard. Tell her if she really loves you she'll go along with it and trust you to do it fairly. And tell her she won't need a lawyer as she can use yours. After all, why pay two different lawyers? If she agrees to this, you're in the clear.

But get the prenuptial agreement! It's easy to get caught up in this love stuff since you probably are in love at the time and she knows it. She'll try her damndest to talk you out of it, and so will her mother and old man. She'll vamp your ass with those pheromones and nylon-clad legs and uplift bras and similar deceptions, so you've got to keep a cool head.

This is one of the first contests of will between you and it's a big one. Be firm. Stand your ground. After all, there's a lot at stake.

Of course, it should be obvious to all but the mentally inept that you don't mention anything about any prenuptial agreements if she's the rich one and you haven't got a dime. Without such an agreement, you'll be able to skin her ass when the divorce comes up and that'll be a refreshing change if nothing else.

SURVIVAL RULES:

1. Remember, no agreement, no wedding. Be firm!
2. Hire a good lawyer, but don't let her have one. Tell her she'll trust you if she loves you.
3. If she has money and you don't, forget the prenuptial agreement. Assume an air of righteous indignation if she insists on one.

Five

SURVIVING THE WEDDING

Okay, so you've done your homework and analyzed her financial assets, discovered her true self, and decided you can live with someone who looks like her mother. Now it's time to get married.

The best advice I can give here is to leave it up to her. All women love weddings and why not? Weddings renew their faith in themselves, in their power over men, in their place in the world. Naturally, they're thrilled to see the grand conspiracy works once more; it gives 'em all hope for their own future.

Did you ever notice people at weddings? All the women are caught up and swept away by the grandeur of it all. They cry and smile sappily and beam at each other and carry on shamefully. But the men? Men look vaguely uncomfortable. They never cry. They grin nervously and flex their shoulders and stare vacantly because they're seeing still another victory for women and defeat for the poor sap busily entangling himself in legal commitments at the altar.

So weddings are for women. Most guys'd just as soon get married by a local judge for twenty bucks and be done with it, but women want something more — a lot more. Well, let 'em have it. Go along

with whatever she and her mother come up with and let her have her moment in the sun. If it all goes smoothly, it may keep the romance in your marriage for another few weeks.

Still, there are caveats. First, make sure her family is paying for it. Don't buy this modern crap that wedding costs should be shared by both families. It's traditional that the bride's family pay for the wedding for the excellent reason that they're unloading a liability and you're taking one on and don't you forget it. The bride pays for the wedding — settle for nothing less.

In fact, since women value tradition so highly, use it to your advantage and insist the wedding vows are traditional ones. Don't let her change to some modern version that limits her duties and obligations and thereby insert an escape clause she can use against you later.

For example, traditional vows assert the woman will "love, honor and *obey*" and most of 'em will suggest dropping that last word since it's no longer appropriate in modern times. Obey stays. Insist on it! Remind her it's traditional and you know how important tradition is to her, and so on.

It's true it won't do any good ultimately, but it'll give you some satisfaction when you can throw it up to her later and demand to know why she doesn't keep her vow to obey her husband as promised.

For the rest, let it go. What color dresses the bridesmaids wear or who sits in which pews or what's served at the reception are questions which only concern the women involved and have nothing to do with you. It's just the first in an endless series of situations where forces outside your control will take over your life and do with it as they will. Get used to it.

There's really nothing more for you to worry about then. Just go with the tide. Try not to get drunk and fall into the wedding cake. Don't make passes at the bridesmaids and try to avoid telling her old lady where to head in.

Hey, it's all over. You're a husband now. Welcome aboard, pal.

SURVIVAL RULES:

1. **Keep the wedding simple if possible, preferably a judge and two strangers for witnesses.**
2. **If that doesn't work, let her and her mother handle the wedding. It's the least you can do.**
3. **Make sure her folks pay for it! Mention tradition and dowries.**
4. **Insist on a traditional service, especially the part about her promising to obey you.**
5. **Try not to insult her mother during the wedding/reception. It gets things off to a bad start otherwise. And don't worry, there'll be plenty of time to insult her ass later.**

Six

WINNING ARGUMENTS

So now you're a married man, a "happily" married man, if you will, and the real challenge is to stay that way insofar as such a thing is possible. And how do you do that?

Easy. Know what's going on and what to do about it.

Let's start with arguments. All married couples argue. They usually start within days of the ceremony, often within hours, and not uncommonly within minutes, and they continue until one of you is dead. It's impossible to avoid arguments so you have to learn how to handle them if you're going to retain even a semblance of control over things.

The crucial argument is the first one. Lose that first argument decisively and you'll set the pattern for the next ten thousand arguments which loom in your future. You *must* either win outright or get a draw. An early defeat is not acceptable, *period*.

Well, how do you insure victory? Just know what's at stake and you'll have an advantage. Most guys don't realize the seriousness of these early arguments and so give in without much resistance. You can always recognize these saps as they're the ones you see meekly enduring public tongue-lashings from their shrewish wives with never the least sign of resistance. We call such wimps henpecked, and there's no sorrier sight on land or sea than a henpecked man.

Okay, so you're having that first argument. Suppose it's over something like, say, your ogling some winsome little creature lounging poolside in about four inches of strategically placed cloth.

"I saw you looking at that girl," she says, pouting.

Now, of course you're guilty. I mean, any guy outfitted with eyeballs would gape at such a sight, but you don't want to admit it because women don't understand such things. So you lie.

"What girl?" you ask, assuming a perplexed look and an air of innocence.

"You know very well what girl!" she retorts. "The one in the green bathing suit. She was lying six feet away from you."

"Oh, her. Was her suit green? Gee, I didn't even realize she was wearing a bathing suit."

"See? You were ogling her!"

"I was not. I never even saw her. I had my eyes closed the whole time."

"Oh, how can you lie like that? We've only been married a week and already you're ogling other girls and lying to me!" She scowls and draws herself up indignantly. "Well, just don't go expecting to get any tonight, that's all I can say!"

Okay, now the gauntlet's been thrown and you've got to stand up and be counted. This is what having balls is all about.

"Oh, yeah?" you say. "Well, I've got news for you, sweetheart. I've got a piece of paper that says I'm entitled to conjugal rights and I'm gonna have 'em, by God!"

"Don't you threaten me! How dare you threaten me? Who do you think you are, anyway? I'll have you know...!" etc.

You don't just get a response, you get a harangue. She's on the attack and gathering steam and you've got to derail her before she steamrolls your ass all the way to henpeckerdom. So you go a little nuts.

"Hey, will you shut up, for Christ's sake?" you shout. "I don't have to take this crap. What the hell's going on here?"

And you kick over a chair and fling the ottoman against the wall and assume a fierce mien and try to create a half-crazy look in your eye so she'll think you're bonkers and be afraid you're going to do her some harm.

Of course, this is all an act. Your anger is controlled anger. You don't actually break things or really hurt anyone, you just want to put the idea in her head for future reference. If you go around breaking out picture windows you'll only have to pay for the damage, but you can create the same effect by, say, tipping over an easy chair or kicking an ottoman. The rest is all acting out the role of a nearly deranged man who mustn't be trifled with for fear he'll go over the edge and throw her down the stairs.

And then you stomp out and go have a drink in a window seat that gives you a good view of the pool and let her simmer. Believe me, when you show up later still wearing a defiant air and look her cooly in the eye, she'll know she's married to a guy with balls, one who'll brook no nonsense. You'll have staked out a claim to your manhood and she'll tread lightly ever after when she rouses your righteous anger.

A word on the use of force, though. No real man ever hits a woman, at least not without major provocation. If some old bat comes at you with a cleaver, you're well within your rights to knock her ass over applecart with a solid right cross, but you mustn't hit her for any lesser reason. It's simply not done, you know.

Wife-beaters are a lowly species and totally without class. No real man will commit such an outrage. If her nagging's driving you crazy, go out and shoot some pool or bowl a few frames, and by the time you come home she'll have run out of gas and shut the hell up. But don't allow yourself to lose your cool and hit her. While it's true enough that she follows no rules whatsoever herself, you've got to rise above her and not allow yourself to sink to her level. After all, you have your dignity, you know.

Another thought. A married man must be prepared to fight to the death wherever and whenever the need arises. She gets an uncontested victory when you refuse to fight back and that's the same as winning the argument on the field of battle. Such practices only serve to embolden the old bat and encourage her to kick your ass just to amuse her girlfriends.

What's more, women are a clever lot and expert connivers. Lots of times they'll try to wear you down with a series of arguments over many months or even years, and the first time you show signs of weakening, bam! they'll strike for the jugular. So spring up on a moment's notice and give her hell and let her know who's in charge and you'll be a helluva lot better off for it in the long run.

Another good tactic when arguing is to throw in such comments as, "Listen, Baby, I love a good fight! You feel like yelling and screaming, well, I'm your man, by God!" and, "If you're looking for trouble, well, you came to the right place, by God! Come on, give me your best shot, Sweetheart! We'll see who's got the balls in this family!" etc.

Once she finds out she can't intimidate you, you've got the battle half won. The old crone'll think twice before riling you up and unleashing a salvo of bile and venom and you'll have a little peace.

Now that isn't to say you should win every argument. A wise man lets the wife win one now and again — but not one that really matters. An argument over who forgot to close the refrigerator isn't very important, but one over whether you can go out with the boys is another story. In other words, pick and choose. Just be sure you win the big ones.

SURVIVAL RULES:
1. **Win the first argument.**
2. **Threaten violence.**
3. **Never beat 'em.**
4. **Never refuse to fight.**
5. **Let her win sometimes...**
6. **...but never the big ones.**

Seven

DEALING WITH IN-LAWS

Most brides come with in-laws, that's a fact and there's nothing you can do about it. Well, how do you deal with 'em? Let's find out.

First, there's a chance your father-in-law will be a decent guy, somebody you might even go fishing with or share a brewski with while watching football, and if that's so, fine. He won't be a problem.

There's a better chance, though, that the old fool will be a pain in the ass and a nuisance to have around. He may regard you as inferior husband material and not nearly good enough for his little girl and drop frequent hints to that effect. Or he may belabor you with unsolicited advice and cadge your cigars and drink up all your Scotch. If so, you'll have to devise a plan to handle the old fraud.

Now the mother-in-law is a horse of a different color. Mothers-in-law are notorious, so much so that they're stereotyped in all societies and cultures. And remember, there's a certain amount of truth in all stereotypes. Her mother will lay waste to your mental well-being and any peace of mind and tranquility you brought to this misalliance.

The reason this is true is because daughter and mother are both females and, therefore, already in cahoots as explained earlier. They've shared a lifetime of common interests and goals. The old lady has spent two or three decades locked in mortal

27

combat with her own husband and knows all the tricks — and she's passed 'em on to her daughter. What's more, she's going to stick around and see 'em put into play.

Okay, what do you do about your in-laws? If there's any hope at all for 'em, you might try conning 'em early on. Compliment the old man on his golf swing or business acumen (if he has any) or war record or whatever. Listen to his windy tales without falling dead asleep in his face and you may be able to win him over and neutralize his ass.

Same with the old lady. Unless she's egregiously ugly, pay her compliments on her looks. Most women are vain beyond belief about their looks and are ready to think well of anyone who tells 'em they're pretty. Or rave about her cooking. Or praise her decorating sense or intelligence or sense of style. In other words, flatter her. There's a chance she'll come to regard you as a real prize and even side with you against her daughter.

But that's not likely to work since she's sure to have a low opinion of your ass the first time she lays eyes on you and will always regard you as a jerk and humbug no matter what you do to convince her otherwise. It never fails. After you've met the family for the first time, there's the inevitable family powwow.

"So, what do you think of him, Mom?" daughter asks.

"Well, he *seems* all right," Mom replies guardedly.

"He's got shifty eyes," Dad harumphs.

"Daddy, he hasn't got shifty eyes!" daughter says.

"Now, dear," Mom says, "it's not his fault. Maybe shifty eyes run in his family."

And it's all downhill from there.

Okay, so what's our plan? Well, there are some tried and true schemes for dealing with in-laws, ideas from antiquity since all ages have suffered 'em. The best plan of all is avoidance.

Stay away from 'em. If possible, move to another state. Or even another country, one without extradition treaties. If you never see 'em, they won't be a problem. You can tolerate anyone if he never comes within a thousand miles of you.

If you can't leave the state, encourage them to do so. Leave retirement brochures touting Sun Belt locations lying around for them to see. Put 'em on mailing lists for the Florida Chamber of Commerce or Sun City condo companies. Give 'em luggage for Christmas.

If all else fails, develop a plan to limit contact as much as possible. Claim their house is full of radon and being there makes you sick. Refuse any evidence to the contrary. If they have a cat, claim you're allergic to cats. Same for dogs or gerbils or even goldfish. Rest assured, if the average woman has to choose between regular visits from her son-in-law and the family pet, she'll choose Fido every time.

What the hell, wouldn't you?

Adopt annoying habits. Smoke enormous black cigars in their house. Cheap ones. Insist you must smoke as it's the only way you can drive out all that

29

radon gas. Light up on the way in and don't let 'er go out until you leave. Smoke at dinner. Drop ashes all over the place and laugh and say they're good for the rugs. That always pisses 'em off.

Get half-loaded on the old man's best Scotch on every visit. Turn on the football game and don't take your eyes off the screen all afternoon. If there's a double-header, watch both games. Insist on eating from a TV table so you won't miss any of the game.

Use the same schemes when they visit you. If they don't like cats, get a couple. Buy a St. Bernard and teach him to slobber all over 'em when they visit. Fill your basement with radon. Smoke incessantly. Hide your good Scotch and serve the old man the deported stuff. After thirty minutes start checking the time and do it again every half-hour until they get the hint and go the hell home.

As effective as all these schemes are, though, your wife will still want some contact with her parents, and rightly so. Well, let her use the phone. Women love phones, they're brought up on 'em and readily accept them in lieu of real life. Put one in some out of the way spot where you won't have to listen to her droning on about nothing for hours at a time and it'll satisfy her completely. You may get some hefty phone bills but that's a helluva lot better than having your in-laws hanging around in person.

Incidentally, if you had the good sense to marry an heiress whose folks own entire landscapes and shipping lines, your in-laws become another matter altogether. In that case, you'll want to cultivate 'em and befriend 'em so they won't cut you out of the will. That means you have to go the flattery and compliments route through sheer necessity. Still, you'll find it's a lot easier to get along with in-laws who insist on showering you with Mercedes coupes and Concorde runs to Paris for the weekend.

So there it is. Lay in a supply of those cheap cigars and light up.

SURVIVAL RULES:

1. **Try to con them with flattery.**
2. **Move to another state if possible or, better yet...**
3. **...encourage *them* to move.**
4. **Try avoidance by making yourself persona non grata around them.**
5. **Encourage your wife to phone her folks and thereby minimize actual contact.**
6. **If your in-laws are rich, forget everything else and go back to rule one.**

Eight

CHILDREN — OPTIONAL

Let's face it, children represent a major crisis in every marriage, and they continue to do so should you elect to have any. Still, at least this is a question you and your wife get to decide for yourselves in this enlightened age and not one that's decided for you by immutable laws of nature.

In olden times people got married and the children appeared every nine or ten months on schedule until the house was full of the little tykes and the woman was broken in health and spirit and finally succumbed. Then the old man would hurry out and find himself a new bride and immediately begin reducing her to mental and physical ruin with eight or ten more kids of her own.

Well, nowadays people make these choices for themselves because modern contraception lets 'em. Lots of people decide not to have children at all in favor of careers and sanity, but it has to be a joint decision and all couples must make it sooner or later.

Okay, let's assume you decide to have 'em. What then?

First, your entire life will be utterly and irreversibly altered forever after. You will stop living for yourself and begin living for your kids. Your every thought will be centered around them and their interests while your own interests and dreams fade into distant memories.

Kids will cause endless problems between you and the missus. She'll insist on raising 'em as believers while you hold out for agnosticism. She'll blame it on your family if they turn out to be losers while claiming all the credit for her side if they turn out to be winners. Your sex life will deteriorate to a point where it would be considered inadequate by the average eunuch. She'll insist you give up cigars on the grounds that they're harmful to the kids and/or the drapes, and she'll nag you to death because you don't earn enough to keep the kids in hundred dollar Nikes.

Think about it.

And another thing, kids are expensive. It's estimated it costs about a hundred grand to raise a kid and get him through one of the cheaper junior colleges. And that's not counting money you'll lay out for such incidental expenses as summer camps, tutors, private schools, new cars, abortions, bail and a host of other costs you never imagined.

You'll need to carry exorbitant insurance and expensive investment plans and give up romantic vacations and drive very old cars and wear stovepipe rack suits and generally live a second-class existence until the last of 'em is grown and living on another continent somewhere.

But that's not the worst of it. The mental costs outweigh even the enormous financial ones. From the time of conception to your own death, you'll worry constantly. You worry because he isn't walking as soon as your cousin's kid. You catch him pulling the cat's tail and worry whether you're raising a psychopath. He flunks pre-school and you're told to plan for his eventual enrollment in meat-cutting school.

His grades are atrocious, his deportment worse. You spend endless hours in the principal's office trying to get his ass reinstated and make repeated trips to court because the half-wit can't drive a car under sixty miles an hour in school zones. He'll likely serve time in various rehab programs for chronic dope smokers; you'll see the day when you're relieved that he's only smoking Camels and getting blotto on beer.

He'll flunk out of college and knock up the neighbor's kid and end up working in fast-food for minimum wage. He'll move back home with his wife and two or three kids and you'll find yourself raising another batch of kids at a time when you should be enjoying the fruits of a lifelong devotion to duty, honor, and parenthood.

Are there any pluses in kids? Of course there are. Lots of kids turn out well, some even becoming model citizens. Kids are nice around Christmas time, they're fun to wrestle with in the evenings before bedtime, and they give you cigars on Father's Day. I've got three of 'em myself and I wouldn't take a million bucks for any one of 'em. Of course, it's also true that I wouldn't give a plugged nickel for another one, either.

So where does that leave you? It leaves you with a decision to make, that's where. It's up to you.

Whatever you do, though, work out the details *before* the wedding. If she wants kids and you don't (or vice versa), decide on a course of action early and avoid major confrontations later. See if you can compromise with a pet. Or maybe annual trips to Europe. Suggest a collection of stuffed toys. Whatever.

Remember, Julius Caesar said, "To have children is to give hostages to Fortune."

Smart dude, ol' J.C.

SURVIVAL RULES:

1. **Kids are**
   a. **optional**
   b. **expensive**
   c. **forever**
   d. **a helluva lot of trouble.**
2. **Kids are also**
   a. **fun**
   b. **your only hope for immortality**
   c. **forever.**
3. **When things go wrong—and they will!—blame your wife. Remember, they're half hers.**

Nine

PICKING THE RIGHT PET

Think about a pet. Sooner or later, the subject will come up and, as always, it's a good idea to plan ahead. If left to your wife, she'll invariably come up with some ridiculous specimen no real man would have around the house.

You know the ones I mean. Those poodles with fancy haircuts, for example. Damn things look foolish. I've even seen neighborhood dogs laughing at 'em when they're out for a walk. *[By the way, there's a euphemism for you. Out for a walk. That's what they call it when you take the critter out so he can crap on somebody else's lawn.]*

Notice I said you. *You* end up walking the hound and you're the sap who has to stand there holding a leash while this ridiculous looking mutt does his business. I mean, if you're going to do the walking, at least arrange to walk a man's dog, for Christ's sake. Put a pit bull on the end of that leash, or a boxer or a doberman, any dog with a little style. Walk a wimpy dog and people'll begin to think you're a wimp yourself.

So plan ahead. What kind of pet would you like? Are you a dog man? Then get yourself a dog before she shows up unannounced with a damn cockatoo or fills the house with cats or gerbils or whatever.

And insist on having only one pet, i.e., yours. Stop by the pound and bring home a mixed breed malamute and present his ass to your wife as a fait acompli.

On the other hand, if you like cats pick one out before your wife beats you to the punch and surprises you with one of those damn yapping little mutts. Get yourself a big cat, one with lots of claws and a mane like a lion, if possible. In fact, you might even get one of those wild cats they sell nowadays. Something like a puma, for example, or maybe an ocelot or a cheetah. Now these are pets a man can be proud of, pets that will make a statement to pet owners everywhere about just who and what you are. Besides, they'll beat the crap out of all the other guys' wimpy cocker spaniels or even their pit bulls, and you'll have every man's honor and respect as a truly macho guy who knows how to pick a pet.

By the way, it's possible you can avoid the whole pet scene if it's really anathema to you by holding out for a pet that's repulsive. Most women hate snakes, for instance, or lizards and tarantulas, so insist on one of these if she starts carping about pets. Tell her you'll get her anything she wants, but you've got to have a foot-wide spider or an eight-foot boa constrictor for yourself. She'll never bring the subject up again.

Another reason for getting a pet your wife doesn't especially care for is to stop her from lavishing affection on the canary that she should be lavishing on you. Once she gets tired of you — a given, of course, in time — she'll look for something else to love and if it isn't the milkman it's sure to be her Inky Poo or Cuddles or Oopsy Wa-wa or whatever.

You've seen the type. Everywhere she goes she's got these ugly Pekingese mutts on a leash and she talks to 'em like they're real people who understand English like a damn native. This babe wouldn't fix a wholesome meal for her old man if her life depended on it, but she cooks exotic foods for Fifi and Doodles. She sees to it that they get weekly pedicures and baths and regular visits to the vet but she doesn't give a damn about her husband's well-being.

Well, if you stick her ass with a ninety pound mixed breed rottweiler and refuse to let her have another pet, she won't want anything to do with the beast let alone waste any affection on it. That way, if anyone in your house gets any haute cuisine, there's a decent chance it'll be you.

If you're not particular what kind of pet you end up with, give some serious thought to a cat. Your wife, or, later, your kids, will eventually want some sort of pet and a cat will be the least troublesome overall.

For one thing, it's easy to housebreak 'em. You take a six week old cat and show him where the litter is and presto! he's trained. That's it. A dog, on the other hand, will piss on every square yard of carpet before the mutt even learns to go on the newspaper you're spreading all over the place. And once he does learn to go outside on other people's lawns, he'll have to be "walked" morning and night in weather both fair and foul and we already know who's going to take him for these walks, remember?

A cat can live on a diet of sparrows and mice provided by nature. All you have to do is supplement 'em with a few kitty kandies and an occasional sprinkling of catnip. A dog, on the other hand, will require hundred pound sacks of dog bones at frequent intervals and generous helpings of raw meat at two bucks a pound.

Also, he'll chew the legs off your Louis XIV couch and eat holes in your mattress, bite the mailman and embroil your ass in lawsuits, piss brown spots all over the lawn, and run away every other day and get picked up by the dogcatcher and you'll have to bail his ass out of the pound at fifty bucks a throw. All in all, a real pain in the ass.

As with everything else, no man needs to suffer these domestic horrors if he'll only plan ahead. It's coming, decisions have to be made, so anticipate 'em. Make the choices early and you'll get to make 'em.

Well, there you have it. One more example of how you can head the old bat off at the pass if you only plan ahead.

SURVIVAL RULES:
1. **You choose the pet — don't leave it to her.**
2. **Get a macho one.**
3. **Don't permit any cute pets — they'll soak up the attention that's rightfully yours.**
4. **Allow only one pet — yours.**
5. **Choose a cat over a dog, they're less trouble.**
6. **Consider a repulsive pet.**

Ten

THE NAGGING WIFE

Think for a minute. How does a ninety-five pound mere wisp of a thing manage to so dominate a guy the size of a pro football linebacker that he cowers like a whipped dog in her presence and lives in terror of her displeasure? I've seen such sights, and so have we all; it's one no man, no real man, ever quite forgets.

Obviously, this guy could stuff the old crone in a handy broom closet and be done with her. Or tell her in a loud voice to shut the hell up and give a man some peace, for Christ's sake. You'd think his physical size alone would assure his supremacy in any kind of contest with a ninety-pound old crone, yet the evidence is there for all to see: She's in charge and they both know it.

Well, how does this happen? How does the old bat pull it off? Easy. She nags his raggedy ass to death, that's how. Most of us have seen nags in action and know what nagging is when we see it, especially if we were raised in a two parent home where all parties necessary to make up a nagging ensemble were available. It goes something like this.

The old man comes home from the VFW hall and there's a slight list to his vertical hold. His wife's voice reaches his ears before she even shows up.

"Where've you been?" she scolds. "Have you been drinking again? I thought you said you were gonna cut down. Didn't you say that? You said you were gonna cut down and you lied. Now, just look at you. What kind of example is that for the children?"

She appears from the kitchen with a cup of coffee in one hand and a jelly donut in the other. She wears a housecoat and stringy hair. The old man grimaces and sidles toward the family room.

"And you stink, too," she goes on. "The whole house stinks of stale beer and... Hey! Is that a cigar you're lighting? I thought I told you no more cigars in the house! My friends come over here and all they can smell is cigar smoke. It's in the drapes and carpets and it sticks to everything. You put that out this very minute or I swear I'll...!"

The old man sheepishly stubs out the newly lit cigar and turns his head as though to lessen the force of a coming blow.

"And don't go turning on any of those stupid football games, either," she rails on. "You watch too much sports, why can't we watch some family shows like General Hospital or Let's Make a Deal or..."

Well, you know the rest. This woman beats this behemoth into jelly solely by talking. She runs her mouth. She narks. She whines. She bitches. She buries his ass in an avalanche of words, piles adjectives on adverbs and nouns on prepositions and verbs on pronouns and stitches the whole oral fabric together with an assortment of commas, dots and dashes, parentheses, quotation marks, semi-colons, question marks, and exclamation points. The only punctuation she never employs is the period.

That's what's called nagging. It's a universal phenomenon that's been around since the late Cretaceous period. History is full of references to its appearance in societies 'round the world. Remember Xanthippe? She drove even so great a figure as Socrates half nuts with her vicious tongue. Did you know that he chose to drink the hemlock instead of accepting exile because the senate decreed he had to take his wife with him? It's the truth, ask any historian.

Isn't that alarming, though? I mean, if one of the greatest minds in the history of the world couldn't deal with a nagging wife, what hope is there for the rest of us? Here you have a man who instructed the world for two and a half millenia and continues to do so today, and yet he allowed his shrewish wife to drive him to an early grave. Jesus.

And how about poor old Abe Lincoln? There have been few greater men in all of history than this remarkable man and yet his life was filled with bitterness and acrimony, and all because he married a shrew who nagged his ass incessantly. We can hardly imagine a kinder, more sympathetic figure than old Abe, but he was putty in his wife's hands because he had no defense against her mouth.

Shakespeare did an entire play about nagging. Remember The Taming of the Shrew? Katherina is nothing more than an old-fashioned nag, a woman with a drill sergeant's tongue and a set of leather bellows for lungs. She gets her way by overwhelming others with sheer volume and wearies 'em to death and ends up a stereotype for nags in literature.

And what about Faulty Towers? Isn't poor old Faulty the epitome of the nagged husband? His wife could serve as a role model for aspiring wives everywhere and Faulty is a pretty good example of the fate awaiting all husbands who succumb.

So is there any hope for us? Of course. Don't forget, Petruchio finally tamed his shrew because he was smarter than Socrates, at least insofar as taming shrews was concerned. And if Petruchio did it, so can you.

The secret once again is to nip it in the bud. First, you must be alert for signs of incipient nagging while still dating, and the first place you're likely to find it is in her own home. In other words, is her mother a nag? If so, we've already seen how daughters mirror their mothers so you can expect the daughter will nag, too.

But what if her mother is clever enough not to let you see that side of her personality and avoids nagging her old man in your presence? How would you know whether she nags then? Easy. Just watch the old man closely. A well-nagged man wears a hang-dog look and evinces a listless spirit completely devoid of any signs of spunk or backbone or balls. He averts his eyes, mumbles noncommital remarks in hopes they won't generate any ire, and often ducks reflexively as though dodging an invisible blow.

If her old man fits this pattern, you can bet his wife reduced him to this state, and that she did it with her tongue. Knowing this, you can either dump her daughter posthaste and avoid having to deal with the problem, or you can go ahead but take the steps necessary to fix it. *Again, I can't overemphasize the need for early treatment.*

Suppose you're dating this girl and you've noticed that she tends to go on a bit about things but she hasn't gotten carried away with it yet because she's still working at keeping you from discovering her true self. So one night you're at your place and she reminds you that you said you'd go with her to, say, her aunt's in Toledo and you don't especially want to go so you've been ducking it.

"I know," she says brightly, "why don't we go see Aunt Helen tomorrow? It's her anniversary and my cousins from Boston will be there and..."

"Nope, bad timing," you say. "Got a meeting down at the VFW hall. Can't miss it. We're gonna blackball Timmy O'Toole."

"But, honey, you said you'd go with me and tomorrow's just perfect because..."

"Hey, what can I do? We're votin'. Everybody's got to be there, it's a rule."

"Well," she says pouting, "I don't see what's so important about one little old meeting. After all, you already spend more time at the hall than you do with me and..."

Okay, so she's starting, right? You've already said you can't go but that isn't good enough for her. She has her mind set on the Aunt Helen trip and she's out to bend you to her will. What do you do?

You sit up and scowl. Practice in the mirror until you get scowling down just right. You want a look that clearly says you're pissed. You need deep furrows in your brow, narrowed eyes, a tightly drawn mouth, and most of all a look in your eyes that shows you mean business, by God!

Look her straight in the eyes and say, "I'll let you know when I'm ready to go."

Keep your eyes locked on hers and stare her ass down. Then get up and go get a cigar and let her know the conversation's over. If you were already married, she'd probably go on with her whining but now she's afraid to make an issue of it for fear of giving herself away. Nine times out of ten she'll back off and you'll have won round one with a knockout.

What about the tenth one? What if she persists and makes an issue of it? Maybe she also knows what's at stake and decides to go for it herself. Dump her. You'll save yourself a lot of headaches later if you just move on and look for a more tractable woman.

Okay, so now you're married and the gloves are off. She starts nagging and you re-enact the scowl and stare routine and the old bat flies into a rage and begins flailing your ass with a torrent of words that sting like so many nettles. Now is the moment of truth arrived, the ultimate test of whether you'll allow yourself to be nagged or not.

You rise up indignantly, scowl fiercely, and say, "Nobody talks to me like that in my own house!"

And then you leave. Get in the car and drive off without a backward glance. Go and don't come back. Stay away. Head for the VFW hall and play some cards, have a few beers, relax. Stay until closing and then curl up on one of the pool tables and spend the night.

Don't call home. You want her to worry. She'll figure she really blew it this time, that maybe she went a tad too far and you may stay away for good. She'll stay up half the night waiting for you but you won't be coming home. And you won't be home the next morning, either. Go straight to work or even take the day off. After work head back to the hall and eat dinner there. Hang out that evening and then go home at ten or so. Just walk in without a word and take your rightful place as the head of your own house and ruler of all you survey.

Don't mention the matter unless she does, and if she brings it up, just frown and say, "I don't want to talk about it." And then don't.

Incidentally, that's one of the most useful phrases in a married man's lexicon. "I don't want to talk about it" has saved more than one guy's ass over the centuries and it'll save yours, too. You see, if there's one thing women like to do it's *talk about it*. Endlessly. In fact, it's what they do best. So it infuriates 'em when you refuse to talk about something, anything.

Yet there's nothing they can do if you refuse to talk. Oh, they can do all the usual stuff like cut you off or refuse to fix breakfast or whatever, but they'll get little real satisfaction from that in the end. I don't mean you refuse to talk at all, by the way, since that's likely to be counterproductive; you just refuse to talk about *that*. It drives 'em nuts.

Anyway, the point is you've established a precedent. She nagged and you put your foot down. Now she knows what to expect in the future. And there will be a next time because she'll test your ass again and again for signs of weakening since all nagging is designed to wear its target down gradually like water eroding granite until it's no longer recognizable as granite.

47

Well, you react the same way each time and storm out of the house in a fit of pique. Stay away longer each time. In time you might even go on week-long fishing trips if she persists long enough. Let her know you'll never give in, that you refuse to allow yourself to be abused in your own house and will never tolerate it no matter what the cost. Eventually, the old bat'll get the message and realize she's married a real man with balls and she's stuck with him.

If you employ this strategy right from the start, you should be able to lead a life free of all nagging and enjoy years of unparalleled peace and tranquility under your own roof. Imagine that. Hell, even Socrates didn't get that, did he?

Amazing.

SURVIVAL RULES:

1. **Nagging is a world-wide phenomenon; women will nag if they can get away with it.**
2. **Your girlfriend is a woman, ergo, she'll nag.**
3. **Pick up on it early; watch her mother.**
   a. Look for signs of the nagged man in her father.
4. **Take a firm stand right at the start and *refuse* to be nagged in your own house.**
5. **Practice scowling, narrowing eyes, etc.**
6. **If she persists in nagging, leave.**
7. **Remember the classic "I don't want to talk about it" ploy.**
8. **Watch for long-term effects. Remember the granite and water analogy.**

Eleven

TOLERATING HER RELIGION

A lot of guys overlook religion when dating a girl and it's easy to do since most of 'em never think about it at any other times, either. I mean, religion doesn't play a prominent role with most guys; at least, if it does, there are few signs of it.

Anyway, this can be one of the worst pitfalls of all. If there's anything more deadly than a wife who loves churches and TV preachers and prayer meetings and other such claptrap, I don't know what it is. A wise man will take to his heels at the first sign of such failings and never look back.

For one thing, these people always hate fun. Check 'em out. Find something most people regard as fun and they'll be dead set against it. They hate dancing and claim it's inspired by Satan. Drinking is taboo, period. Cigars are evil incarnate and a sure path to perdition. Pool is verboten, dancing girls off-limits, X-rated movies immoral. Playboy and Penthouse drive 'em nuts. Even swearing is frowned upon, for Christ's sake.

How can you live with such people?

Marry one of these broads and you'll spend the next forty years surrounded by a lot of lackluster sods wearing cheap suits and holier-than-thou airs. Your house will be filled with religious pamphlets and the sound of TV evangelists exhorting you to send money. You'll come home from work and find your wife has invited a tribe of Seventh Day Adventists in for a chat and they'll harangue you for hours on end and urge you to repent and live a life of dreariness like them.

Incredible.

Well, how do you protect yourself against this calamity? Remember, while you're dating she's artfully concealing her true self from you lest you find out what she's really like and dump her. I mean, if your girlfriend starts nagging and gains forty pounds and orders you to give up cigars before you're legally tied up, you'll tell her to get lost and go find another girl and she knows it. So she plays a waiting game, misleading you with small deceptions and even outright lies and conning you into believing she's something she's not. You don't begin to see her real self until after the wedding.

But the signs are there. For example, maybe she wears a cross around her neck. That's not a good sign. You'll rarely see a cross on a real fun-loving type of girl and that's the kind you want, isn't it? So if she wears a cross, check her out.

Sneak over on Sunday morning and follow her. See if she goes to church — and what kind of church she goes to. If she shows up at one of those evangelical tents thrown up on a vacant lot somewhere, drop her ass on the spot. It's already too late to help her; she's fallen in with an undesirable lot and is beyond saving.

The store-front variety of church is another dead giveaway. Drop her. Cathedrals are a bit better as Catholics are usually not as extreme in their beliefs

— they can go to confession and clean the slate every year or so and this gives 'em a little leeway. Exotic churches are risky, too, because a lot of 'em have strange rituals and attract a lot of garlic eaters.

The bottom line is, if she goes to *any* church on a regular basis, you may be in trouble.

There are other signs, too. One is a reluctance to give you any. A lot of these women actually believe sex is against some kind of moral law or something and fear retribution if they give it up before marriage. This is definitely not a good sign. Women who think that way often regard sex itself as evil and they never put their whole heart into it even after they've had the act blessed by all the church elders in a public ceremony.

Other signs? Prudishness. Tell an off-color joke and watch her reaction. If she scowls she may be a closet religioso. Leave your copy of Playboy lying around where she can see it. Hang some centerfolds on your bedroom walls. Display your collection of X-rated statuary. Keep a bowl of condoms on your coffee table. If she evinces any antipathy toward these things, be on your guard.

Better yet, take her to a girly show. Stop by the local topless bar for a drink one night and gauge her reaction to all the bare boobs. Or rent some X-rated flicks for a Saturday night and watch 'em together. Keep a close eye on her for any signs of revulsion. You can even go a step further and see if she's willing to recreate any of the action on the screen, or even whip out your own camcorder and offer to immortalize her on film. If she takes these

51

things in stride, chances are you'll have little to fear in terms of her being some kind of religious nut.

But suppose she's an especially cunning and crafty woman who manages to keep her darker side hidden from you and you find you've got a full-blown Holy Roller on your hands after the wedding. In that case, counter mysticism with more of the same. Tell her you've been a secret voodooist all along and show her your collection of pinned dolls and chicken feathers dipped in red ink to simulate blood. Leave mysterious writings around the house and pick up some satanist literature to scatter around for her benefit.

Insist that she respect your religion just as you respect hers. Remind her we're a pluralistic society with room for everyone's particular brand of craziness and all are to be equally valued. If she continues to rail against your sacred beliefs, sic the ACLU on her ass, by God.

Whatever you do, though, don't ever give in. Don't even humor her. Once the Holy Rollers get you in their clutches, you're a goner every time. You'll end up leading a colorless and empty life, one entirely devoid of fun and gaiety and charm. There is no grimmer fate.

Well, don't worry about it. Any sensible guy can avoid the whole scene just by making damn sure he doesn't hook up with a religious nut to start with. They're easy to spot; all one has to do is keep his eyes open and pay attention.

SURVIVAL RULES:

1. Look for signs of excessive moral fibre.
2. Resist all attempts to make you give up your vices.
3. If she has to have some religion, let her be Unitarian. They're more liberal than some of the others.
4. If you end up stuck with a Holy Roller, counter by claiming membership in some exotic faith which requires unremitting sinning.
5. Never go with her to church unless she agrees to go to your satanic/voodooist services, as well. She won't.

Twelve

CONTROLLING THE MONEY

Okay, now the big question. What's the story on money? If there's a likely source for future trouble, this is it. Arguments over money cause more marital discord and strife than any other single problem. It's easily one of the leading causes of divorce, one that pisses off more people than almost all others combined.

Well, what are some things you can do to minimize money woes in your marriage? For one thing, you can pick a wife who handles money sensibly. And how do you do this? Easy. By paying attention before marriage.

When dating, watch her. How does she handle money? Is she always broke? Are her credit cards maxed out ninety percent of the time? Does she know the UPS truck driver by his first name? Does she nag you for expensive gifts? Is she a mall freak? Is her mother a spendthrift?

Old habits die hard. If your intended spends money like the proverbial drunken sailor before you marry her, she'll do it after, too. Keep a sharp eye peeled for signs of profligacy and dump her if you find any.

On the other hand, if she's too tightfisted with her money she'll be a penny pincher later, too. That might be okay on the one hand, but it could mean she'll bitch and whine every time you play a round of golf or lay in a new supply of cigars. There's nothing worse than being married to a woman who's a tightwad and laments every outlay of cash that isn't directly required for survival.

What you want, of course, is someone in the middle. Ideally, a woman with a healthy savings account and a good stock portfolio who also likes to have a good time and doesn't mind spending for it. This kind of woman is not available everywhere, of course, but it's a goal you should set for yourself.

How do you find out which type your proposed bride is? Hint around. Bring up a discussion of stocks and bonds. Trick her into a conversation centered around balancing checkbooks and if she doesn't know what the hell you're talking about, dump her. See if she watches Wall Street Week. Has she ever heard of the Wall Street Journal? Is her car paid for? Does she try to borrow money from you?

Or is she a cheap tipper? Does she have money and still drive an eleven year old car? Does she buy you cheap gifts? Or *any* gifts? In other words, open your eyes and take a look around and ask yourself, "Is this girl a bargain or not?"

Another thing, remember that we've become a nation where two incomes are required and wives are expected to work. Has she got any skills? Is she an MD or a lawyer or, even better, an heiress? Make the right choice here and you may be able to lead a life of leisure while your wife hauls in a substantial income all by herself. You might even be one of these stay-at-home husbands we hear so much about lately and spend your days shooting pool and tying fishing flies.

But marry some unskilled lout whose idea of a career is delivering pizzas and you'll end up working two jobs yourself and never see the inside of a pool hall again. Be smart, plan ahead.

In any case, once you're married there are certain things you can do to insure an even break in the final distribution of family income. For openers, you handle the finances. I don't give a damn if you're a football coach and your wife's a C.P.A. who works as a financial planner. *You* handle the finances. Remember, whoever controls the purse strings controls everything else.

The first thing is to squirrel away a private bank account for your own use. Slip x-number of dollars out of every paycheck and bank it. It'll come in handy for that new shotgun you'll want some day or season tickets for your favorite football team. When you need it all you do is claim you won the office pool or enjoyed some other windfall and presto! you're off to the gun shop to pick up your new hand-carved double-barrel shotgun complete with racing stripe and anti-locking gears.

You may rest assured that the wife'll have a little account of her own, too. Most wives are instinctive embezzlers adept at diverting money into their own private accounts. They've always done so. A lot of 'em are saving up to run away, and if the husband knew it he'd write 'em a check to help them reach their goal sooner.

Consider the opposite approach, though, the one where your wife handles the money. Not only is she in a position to embezzle all the more freely, but she knows what happens to every penny you get. Buy a round of drinks for the boys and she knows it. Lose a bit at golf and you get a lecture on the evils of gambling. Take a comely colleague to lunch and she gets the credit card receipt.

What's even worse, you end up on what's known as an "allowance". You work your ass off all week and turn your paycheck over to the little woman in toto. She does the banking and gives you, say, twenty bucks for expenses, (i.e. gas, lunches, cigars, booze, etc.). Two days later the twenty's gone and you have to creep hat in hand and ask Miss Shylock for more of your own damn money!

"What'd you do with the money I gave you on Thursday?" she demands.

"I bought gas," you say.

"Gas doesn't cost twenty dollars."

"Hey, I bought some cigars, too."

"Didn't you just buy cigars the other day? You smoke too much. Do you realize you spend three dollars a day on cigars? Do you know how much that would add up to at the end of a year? I think you should cut down and..."

See? Little Billy asking mommy for his allowance. Isn't that a disgraceful scene? You bet your ass it is — and it's one you can avoid just by keeping her away from the family till.

Another thing, wives go nuts with this shopping business. Show 'em a sale and they salivate like Pavlov's dogs. They can't help it. Most women are

"YOU'LL BE HAPPY TO KNOW I'M RAISING
YOUR ALLOWANCE THIS MONTH."

susceptible and utterly without resistance. I remember when my own mother, a stout Baptist who shunned all alcohol, loaded a six pack into her shopping cart and when I pointed out she was buying beer she said, "Oh. Well, it was on sale."

This weakness manifests itself in enormous bills from the Visa people. Half the households in America are on the brink of bankruptcy and it's usually the fault of the wife and her inability to resist temptation. Give the old bat complete access to your finances and she'll reduce you to penury in nothing flat.

By the way, unscrupulous merchants even prey on women in their own homes these days. They do it with catalogues. The damn things arrive by the carload and they're wreaking havoc across the land. Even the postal people are pissed because an epidemic of hernia cases has struck their workers in recent years. The poor bastards have to carry mail bags weighing more than they do and it's taking a toll on 'em.

Anyway, don't let 'em in your house. When the first catalogue shows up, throw it away. Tell your wife it's a personal quirk. Tell her all the sexy models these mags feature arouse you sexually and cause you to think impure thoughts and masturbate excessively or whatever. Make her vow never to have 'em around or even glance through 'em. If you take a firm stand right from the very start, your wife will never acquire the deadly catalogue virus which has ruined so many of your fellows.

But you get the point by now. If you value your sanity, your net worth, your freedom — your very life, even! — don't let her get her lunchhooks on your bank account. Most women are really unfit for the responsibilities of fiscal management, anyway, and actually prefer to have the man do it. Everybody knows that.

Ergo, you must handle the money to save her from herself. Believe me, some day she'll thank you for it.

SURVIVAL RULES:

1. You handle the money!!
2. Remember, money is the chief cause of domestic strife.
3. Marry an heiress, if possible.
4. Marry a woman with good money sense and good earning potential.
5. Avoid women who are skinflints.
6. You handle the money!!
7. Build up a secret slush fund for emergencies.
8. Never accept an "allowance".
9. Keep a tight rein on her spending. Keep temptation from her — no catalogues, etc.
10. You handle the money!!

Thirteen

LIFE INSURANCE?

Sometime shortly after the wedding, usually during a lull in honeymoon activities, your new bride will deftly bring up the subject of insurance.

"Mother lost her suitcase when she flew home," she'll say one day. "But she had it insured so she's lucky, isn't she? I told her to insure it and she didn't want to but then she did and now she's glad." Pause. "By the way, do you have any life insurance, honey?"

There. Already she's laying plans for your demise — and for ways to profit from it when that day comes. The fact that you have no children yet and she's in perfect health and well able to care for herself is irrelevant. She wants a windfall when you croak and she's going to get it.

Women love life insurance and men hate it. In the first place, we usually wind up having to pay for the goddam stuff but that isn't the only reason we don't like it. The truth is we never get to spend it. Women outlive us by eight or ten years and they know it. They're the ones who end up spending life insurance so they have a vested interest in the stuff.

Notice that single people don't carry life insurance since they know they won't be spending it. Nobody feels responsible for the financial well-being of anyone else and leaves it up to him to provide for his own old age. Well, the same principle applies to a guy with a new wife who's able to take care of herself. If he croaks, she'll just go on working — and looking for her next husband.

Well, by God, I say let her look for the next one with her own money. I'm damned if I want to finance the venture.

Besides, remember you've only just married this woman. How do you know she isn't a vicious predator who goes around insuring new husbands just so she can poison 'em and run off with the insurance agent? After all, you hardly know her. She's already deceived you on a hundred other things so why can't she hide the fact that she's a modern-day Lucretia Borgia?

So refuse to buy life insurance at least long enough to ascertain her real intentions. Tell her it's an unsound investment, that you'd rather put your money in good mutual funds and reap the rewards of their growth. Of course, you don't actually have to buy any mutual funds as long as she thinks you will someday. That way you can blow those insurance premiums on sensible things like custom-made pool cues and nifty fishing boats and similar stuff you'll enjoy now instead of salting the money away to enrich her when you're gone.

And you can always fall back on the old religion dodge if cornered. Claim adherence to some obscure religious sect that thinks insurance is against God's will. Insist that God will provide. Tell her the biblical story about the sparrow falling and all that. It'll keep her off balance and save you a fortune on premiums.

Of course, if you have kids you'll have to forgo such luxuries as pool cues and fishing boats and buy insurance by the ton. That's what comes of having kids. You'll need at least a million or so to cover the costs of their college educations at Harvard and retire the mortgage on the house so they won't end up living in cardboard boxes on the streets.

In any case, forewarned is forearmed. You don't want to end up in the next edition of True Detective with gruesome pictures of cops exhuming your remains for traces of arsenic and lurid details of how you were one of a score of victims who fell for the old insure 'em and knock 'em off scam.

As I said, you never know.

SURVIVAL RULES:

1. **Avoid life insurance.**
2. **Remember, you don't get to spend it.**
3. **If she presses the issue, tell her your faith prohibits insurance.**
4. **Trick her; offer to invest in lieu of insurance.**
5. **If you have kids, do the right thing and sign up.**

Fourteen

AVOIDING HOUSEWORK

Another pain in the ass is all this housework crap. There isn't a wife on Earth who doesn't whine and bitch because her husband won't help with the housework. And even if he does, she's never satisfied and thinks he doesn't do enough.

All right, maybe they've got a case in some ways. I mean, hell, housework is a drag and, what's more, it's unmanly. Wearing an apron and wielding a featherduster isn't the Marlboro man image most guys have of themselves, is it? What young kid grows up picturing himself scrubbing pots and vacuuming rugs? Do you think Ernest Hemingway started like this? Or Humphrey Bogart? Or any guy with balls?

Once more, the secret is taking early action. Know the enemy and take steps to thwart the bastard before it's too late. There are several courses of action open to you, all more or less effective, but only if carefully established in the very beginning.

One is the old war-injury ploy. The very first time she asks you to move the couch, say, or climb a ladder to hang curtains, beg off on the grounds of said injury.

"Gee, honey," you say, "I'd love to give you a hand but I've got this shrapnel in my knee and..."

What can she say, for Christ's sake? You're a damn wounded war hero. What woman can be such an ungrateful bitch that she won't respect a man who was crippled while defending his country against her enemies?

If you weren't in the war, lie about it. Tell her it happened on the grenade range when you threw your body on a live grenade to save your buddies. Everybody likes that one. Or, if you weren't even in the army, make it an old football injury. Women love those, too. Tell her again how you caught the winning touchdown pass in the Orange Bowl with two seconds left and a three hundred pound tackle on your neck. She'll believe you since she probably doesn't know a thing about football or the Orange Bowl or anything else connected with sports.

Remember, though, liars need good memories. If you tell her the grenade story, don't forget next time and make it a mortar shell. Women can be duped but they're not stupid, and she'll catch you every time if you slip up.

And remember that you've got to be consistent. If you claim a bad knee, don't let her see you scampering lithely over the tennis courts on two good knees. She'll get suspicious and wonder what happened to all that shrapnel you were talking about.

Another scheme that works is to claim you're allergic to all cleaning compounds, window solvents, dust balls, vacuum handles, wallpaper paste, and so on. In fact, you can even claim your allergies kick in just by being in the vicinity when such things are being used and that will give you an excuse to go play golf or shoot some pool when *she's* doing the housework. And it also means you won't have to sit around feeling guilty as she scrubs the floors and reposititions the refrigerator because you won't even be there! Isn't that beautiful?

Or you can use religion again. Tell her you're a Muslim and the Koran forbids men from doing such work. Offer to do any real man's work that needs being done. Are there camels that she wants driven to market? Or goats rounded up? Does she need something from the local coffee house where you're required to spend six hours a day playing cards? No problem. But housework is out of the question since you aren't about to incur the wrath of the gods by doing the dishes.

Then again, there's another side to this question, one we should consider if we're being completely fair here. Since your wife will doubtless have a job and work eight hours a day outside the home just as you do, it may be only right that an enlightened husband makes some effort to share household duties at least on some level. But have a care!

Give her an inch and you could end up nominated for spineless wimp of the year. Many a man has agreed to sweep off the stoop in a weak moment and found himself a full-time maid and handyman before he knew what the hell was going on.

So she has a point. I mean, if you're both working outside the home it's reasonable that you both share equally in the housework, right? It's a damn good argument, one that's hard to refute. Okay, there's a way to deal with this, too.

Do it but do it badly. If she says wash the windows, leave 'em streaked. Knock over her prized geraniums while climbing around the outside windows. Fall off the ladder and claim you hurt your back.

"I CHANGED MY MIND, YOU CAN GO BACK
TO WATCHING YOUR FOOTBALL GAME."

Vacuuming? Bang things with the vacuum. Scar up her antique Chippendale chair legs. Never empty the bag. Miss big balls of lint on purpose.

Make the bed with the spread upside down. Fold the sheets up in a big ball when putting the laundry away. Chip a piece or two of her crystal and she'll never ask you to wash the glasses again. Knock over lamps when you dust. Slop water all over the kitchen wallpaper when she makes you do the floors. Forget to feed the cats for days on end and she'll stop asking you to do it.

There you have it. It's a universal rule, at home or work or in the army or wherever, if you screw something up, people'll stop asking you to do it. So pitch in and do it willingly, even smilingly. Show a cheery outlook and a real interest in compromising, but screw it up. In no time, she'll write your ass off as a hopeless incompetent and take over all the chores herself.

So as long as she's working you agree to do some of the housework because you're a nice guy. But when the first kid shows up and she stays home to be a full-time mother and homemaker, all bets are off. There's no longer any need for subterfuge or malingering, no need for arguments or strife; she does it all alone and that's the end of it.

In spite of what women would like you to think, they lead lives of indolence and ease when they stay home. Consider the facts. Let's say you're one of these new-fangled house-husbands we hear so much about. You've got a new month-old kid and you're raising him while the wife works.

Let's take a look at your day. Your wife rises at six-thirty and gets ready for work. She fixes her own breakfast, of course. (What homemaker in America fixes her husband's breakfast? Such a thing is unheard of.) She leaves for work at eight and you're on your own.

Now for the first few months you'll be doing the night feeding thing and it's a pain, but you can get the little guy to sleep through the night by the time he's three or four months old at the latest, especially if you slip him a Mickey with his last bottle. A few drops of your Scotch in his milk and he'll sleep like, well, a baby.

Okay, so you feed junior his six o'clock bottle, change him, and tuck him back in bed. Now it's eight and your wife's gone. You clean up the kitchen. What's this? Six minutes? Maybe eight? You put two cups and a cereal bowl in the dishwasher and sponge up some toast crumbs. Big deal.

Next, you vacuum. You can vacuum a nine room house in twenty minutes, tops. I know because I live in a nine room house and I once did it myself. Then what? The laundry? Okay. Separate the light and dark stuff, toss in a handful of soap, and press some buttons. Four minutes flat. Make the bed. Two minutes, three if you stop to play with the cat.

There you are. Eight-thirty and you're done. Turn on the TV, snuggle in with the morning paper, and that's it until ten when junior gets his next bottle. The rest of the day is yours. You can talk on the phone to your hard working homemaker friends in the neighborhood, read a good book, drink coffee, sleep, whatever. Aside from an occasional bottle for junior, your time's your own.

Oh, sure, I know windows need washing once in a while and floors need scrubbing and whatnot, but these aren't daily chores. We're looking at a typical average day in a so-called homemaker's life, and this is what we see. I've made a study of it and I can tell you there isn't more than four hours' worth of work a week in keeping up a fairly large home.

Want proof? Rig up your camcorder. Focus the thing on the chair she watches TV from. Wire the house. Arrange little traps designed to catch her in the act. Lean something against the vacuum cleaner to see if it's been moved during your absence. Write the date in the dust on the buffet. Keep notes on what you're served for dinner each day and see if you don't get a lot of TV dinners, reheated leftovers, grilled cheese sandwiches and canned soup. You'll have concrete evidence that would stand up in a court of law and defy cross-examination by Perry Mason himself.

Yet in spite of this, your wife has the gall to ask you to help out around the house! Well, by God, don't you do it! You tell her straight out it's her job and you don't want to hear any more about it. You work at the office and she does the house, period. No more of this job-jar crap. No list of chores waiting to screw up every weekend. No more whining and bitching about being overworked. The matter's resolved.

As I said, it's one thing if she works outside the home, but you draw the line on her ass when she quits her job. If she's going to play house all day while you slave away your life over a hot computer or drill press, then let her have it all, by God.

SURVIVAL RULES:

1. **Housework is unmanly; don't do it.**

   a. **Claim an old war (football, etc.) injury prevents your doing housework.**

   b. **Assert you're a Muslim and the Koran forbids men doing housework.**

2. **Claim allergies to cleaning solvents, etc.**

3. **If all else fails, do it but screw it up.**

4. **When she quits her job to stay home, all bets are off. She does all the housework, period.**

Fifteen

FEMINIST WIVES

Your wife is one of these. Oh, she may deny it but she's in the clan, all right. They are feminists because it lets 'em have the best of all possible worlds. They demand equal rights with men — and get 'em, too — and still insist on their womanly prerogatives. What the hell, that's such a good deal you'd join up yourself if you could.

Well, this will have some bearing on your home life. I mean, if she's reading Ms. Magazine and bitching about her rights all day, it's likely to redound to your harm. The feminist movement has been the undoing of many an otherwise happy marriage and yours could well be the next one to go.

To be honest, though, this idea made sense a few years ago when women realized they were getting the short end of the stick, so to speak, in a lot of things. They weren't being paid enough, they didn't get promoted, they were denied access to a lot of jobs they could perform perfectly well, they couldn't go into all-male clubs and play pool with the guys, and whatnot. They said all this was discriminatory and they were right.

So we fixed all that. Now they can play pool anywhere they damn well please, they're routinely promoted, often just to meet quotas, and they work at everything from deep-sea diver to test pilot and have become man's equal in every way. Yet they're not happy.

And why aren't they happy? Because they've found out it's no fun working at some dreary job for some ignoramus of a boss who underpays 'em and browbeats 'em and drives 'em half nuts eight hours a day. Rush hour traffic and deadlines and abuse and internecine warfare with their colleagues and missed promotions and all the rest of it have soured a lot of 'em on the whole feminist idea. Look how the E.R.A. thing went down a few years back. All of a sudden everybody's got doubts; the thing's gone full cycle and doubled back on 'em.

What's all this mean to you? For one thing, it means your wife will get tired of the grind and start dropping hints about her biological clock running down on her. She'll do this even if she's only twenty-two because it's chic to talk about biological clocks these days. They say it's because they want to fulfill their destiny as women and nurture small infants when it's really because they want to stay home and watch TV.

Well, don't let her get away with it. Insist that she keep her nose to the corporate grindstone until her biological clock's reached the eleventh hour. You need her income to keep up the payments on the two cars and the new Tudor you're building. If she quits you'll have to trade your Volvo 770 Superliner in for a used Chevette and ditch the house for an asbestos-sided bungalow in Nowheresville.

If she gives you too much static, remind her that there's no longer any alimony, thanks largely to the feminist movement. No-fault divorce gave women equality, all right, and it also took away a few goodies they once held so dear. It's no longer possible for them to marry some poor sap and then divorce his ass and continue to make him pay for his mistake for the rest of his life. There's a bit of justice they hadn't counted on.

It's best to start undermining her feminist ideas right away. Hide Ms.Magazine on her. Leave articles around that assert all feminists are lesbians. Refuse to watch TV shows that glamorize women who burn their poor husbands to death while they're dead drunk and unconscious and then beat the rap in a trial run by wild-eyed liberals who can't tell first degree murder from self-defense when they see it. Use Betty Freidan's picture as a dartboard in the rec room. In these and other equally subtle ways, let the old bat know you don't approve of feminism and will not abide it in your house. Fail to do this and it may not be your house at all before long.

The main thing is to hold onto whatever power you can in this lifelong struggle they call marriage. You can bet your ass that your wife is scheming night and day to turn you into a jellyfish so she can have things done her way and it's up to you to resist her machinations as best you can.

Remember what's at stake. We're talking life and death here, a fight you can't afford to lose. Ask no quarter and give none, but be sure you have at least a quarter to negotiate with.

SURVIVAL RULES:

1. **Many women are feminists.**
2. **They want it both ways — and usually get it, too.**
3. **Resist 'em, refuse to countenance it, especially in your own house.**

Sixteen

BOYS' NIGHT OUT

Picture this scenario. A guy and his wife are watching TV of an evening when the phone rings. The guy answers it.

"Hi, Jack, what's up? Bowling, eh?" Looks apprehensively at his wife's back. "Tom can't make it? You need a sub, eh?" Listens and chews lip nervously. "Uh, yeah. Just a minute, Jack. Hold on." Turns to wife. "Uh, honey, it's Jack. Tom can't make it tonight and the guys need a sub. I figured I could fill in and..."

"No," she says flatly. "You went out last month."

"But, gee, honey, that was for Ed Hashimoto's funeral!" he whines.

"I said no. They can just get someone else to fill in."

The guy glares at her back and takes a step forward as he raises the phone over his head, then he reverts to his true character and speaks into the phone. "Uh, sorry, Jack, I, uh, my wife is, uh... Yeah, sure. Maybe next time. 'Bye."

He hangs up and slinks spiritlessly back into his chair and stares moodily at the TV.

Isn't that disgusting? Why, he should brain the old crone with the goddam phone and go bowling with the boys. There isn't a jury in the land that'd convict him, by God.

The question is, how did this poor slob reach this awful state? Why does a two hundred pound stevedore let his hundred pound wife beat him into such total submission and never so much as whimper? Can such a thing happen to you? You're damn right it can, and it will, too, if you don't watch your ass.

You see, nobody starts out like that. This isn't a subject that comes up for discussion before the wedding because she's still got you vamped out of your damn skull with all this "love" crap and you aren't thinking rationally. You just assume you'll continue to bowl with the team or play hockey at midnight or enjoy the monthly poker game with the boys. After all, haven't you done all these things routinely for the last six or seven years?

Of course you have. And you will after you're married, too. It goes without saying, as they say. Well, I've got news for you. The dope in our little scenario once entertained such thoughts and look at him now. He's a beaten man, a man without spirit or spunk; in brief, he's a man without a boys' night out.

The truth is, no man is entitled to a regular night out by some kind of divine right; nights out are earned, taken, seized, usurped; they're never given because no wife'd ever consent to such a thing of her own volition. If she had her way, she'd have your ass assigned to permanent house arrest and hang those electronic gadgets the police use now to keep tabs on crooks all over your hide.

Why do wives feel that way? Because they're insecure, that's why. They're afraid if you get out there on your own and meet real people and have some fun you'll never come back. And how can you blame 'em considering the lives most of their husbands lead at home. The local pool hall can seem a helluva lot cheerier place than a family room presided over by a mean-spirited, cantankerous old bat who finds pleasure in crushing a man's spirit.

So you've got to plan early and well. Long before there's any talk of weddings, let her know that Wednesdays are racquetball or bowling night or whatever and every other Friday is poker night with the guys. These nights are inviolable. Never skip one to do anything with her. If she makes plans for a Wednesday or poker night, you refuse to go. Since she hasn't tangled you up in legal knots yet, she'll be reluctant to issue any ultimatums and decide to humor you until after the wedding.

But you've read this guide; you're ready for her. On the first Wednesday after the honeymoon, grab your bowling bag or racquet and head for the gym.

Don't ask her if you can go!

That's fatal. Once she gets even the seed of an idea that she can prevent your going, the jig's up. You assume you can go, act as though it's a given. If she questions it, assume a cool air and smile a little smile, a patronizing smile. Practice in the mirror to make sure you've got it down just right.

"Where are you going, honey?" she asks.

Smile. "It's Wednesday, Sugar," you say, and head for the door.

"But I thought we'd go see Mother tonight," she pouts.

"Not on Wednesdays, dear."

Bam! That's it. You're gone, case closed. What if she raises a hue and cry and creates a scene and vows to cut you off? You scowl the fiercest scowl you can muster (practice in the mirror until you get it down just right) and let her know in no uncertain terms that nothing gets in the way of racquet-ball/bowling/whatever.

Remind her that you pay x-dollars a month for the club and don't believe in wasting money by not using the facilities. Point out how necessary the activity is for your health. Suggest that she accompany you if she'd like — and don't worry, she won't. The last thing she wants is to hang around some smelly old gym watching people sweat.

Then leave. And leave every Wednesday night even if the damn gym's closed for repairs. Go hang around the corner if you have to, but don't break the pattern no matter what. Before long she'll get used to your nights out and won't question them. They'll become a part of the very fabric of your marriage, a constant, unchanging factor accepted by one and all. It just takes a little planning and the balls to stay the course.

By the way, if you're a war vet you might want to join the local VFW or American Legion post as these are excellent night out spots. They're open just about every night and the chief activities are drinking, smoking cigars, and swapping apocryphal war stories with your fellow members. Beats the hell out of sweating your ass off in some stuffy gym.

If you're not a vet another good club is one of these Knights of Columbus outfits. They'll take anybody who claims to be a Catholic though actual church membership and participation isn't required. If it were half the KC halls in the damn country would close down overnight. The activities are the same as those in Legion posts.

Well, wherever you go, the object is to go someplace so you can get out of the house and get some peace and quiet for a change. Togetherness is great in the abstract, but it can get old pretty quick in a marriage. Everybody needs time away from his wife, even guys who still like theirs.

A guy needs time for manly things, too. You know, macho guy stuff with a lot of cigar smoking and spitting and sports talk and dirty jokes and all the rest. All these activities are frowned upon by wives everywhere, though, and they'll do whatever they can to keep you from 'em.

If you're paying attention, you'll know how to beat 'em at their own game and enjoy a kind of wedded bliss seldom seen in these parts.

SURVIVAL RULES:
1. **Set patterns *before* marriage.**
2. **Nights out are earned, not given.**
3. **Join a club, preferably one that features cigars and booze.**
4. **Keep nights out inviolate.**
5. **Never ask if you can go out!**
6. **Practice patronizing smiles.**

Seventeen

PRESERVING YOUR VICES

Now if your wife's like all the others, she'll start in modifying your habits before the ink is dry on the license. She's long since apprised herself of your faults and defects, and if she missed any her old lady was sure to point 'em out. She weighed these defects to see if they were serious enough to dump you over and, deciding they weren't went ahead with the wedding.

Of course, you also spotted some defects of hers but you're like most guys and willing to allow a few deficiencies here and there as long as the overall package is in fairly good shape. Not so women, though. No woman is ever satisfied with the slightest defect in her husband and will move Heaven and Earth to correct every last one of 'em.

Oh, she starts off innocently enough. On your honeymoon you'll sit down and light up a genuine deported Cuban cheroot and find a magazine opened to an article on the dangers of smoking lying on the table next to the ashtray. It'll probably be illustrated with graphic pictures of blackened lungs and poor saps hooked up to oxygen tanks with ex-Surgeon General Koop's picture scowling at you.

You'll ignore it, of course, and rightly so since something gets everybody in the end, anyway, so what's the difference? (Something's even creeping up on the smug Dr. Koop but he doesn't know it.) Next she'll be sitting windward of your cheroot and you'll catch her frowning and making a show of waving the smoke away from her face. Ever the gentleman, you offer to move to the lee side and give her some respite. But that isn't good enough for Little Miss Reformer Of Other People's Habits.

Now notice. You've been polluting the air around her for a year or more with never a whimper out of her. Even her mother has kept her own counsel about your cigars. But you're married now and all of a sudden they bother her. They smell now. Pretty soon they stink. Before you know it, they'll be affecting her asthma (which she forgot to mention she had, by the way) and are harming her health.

Next she starts carping on the subject. She criticizes your smoking too early in the day, or during meals, or in public places, and finally *at all*. She starts complaining about the cost, the ashes, and what the neighbors will think. After a while all this crap begins to wear you down and, since you're a decent chap and interested in peace and harmony, you begin to cut down on your smoking, finally even hesitate to light up when she's within hailing distance, and at last she succeeds in pounding you into emotional rubble and you give up the practice altogether.

There. She's done it again. Reordered someone else's life to suit her own, deprived a guy of a small pleasure out of pure meanness.

Appalling.

What can you do? Resist. Refuse to give in. Be defiant, even. Find ever bigger cigars, fat, black ones, cheap ones. Include scented cigars that smell of burning rubber and old rags. Hide dead cigar butts around the house and leave the wrappers and bands on the floor where they fall. Smoke 'em in her car with the windows up when she's not looking and leave the butts under the seat.

After a while one of two things will happen. She'll either flip out altogether and fly the coop or her olfactory, optical, and asthmatic nerves will short out entirely and leave her immune to cigar smoke. In either case, you'll be able to puff away to your heart's content and revel in retained manhood. Hooray!

The same principles apply to your other vices. If you like to drop by the track now and then, it'll piss her off eventually and she'll start a campaign to prevent it. Don't let her. Subscribe to the Racing Form and read it at breakfast. Invite some of your sleazy race track buddies to come by for a beer and fill the house with bad English and loud suits. Pick up losing fifty buck tickets at the track and leave 'em in your coat pockets to freak her out even more. Refuse to have anything to do with Gamblers Anonymous but encourage her to go to meetings for Wives of Anonymous Gamblers as it'll get her ass out of the house once a week.

Now drinking is another matter. You've got to be careful with this one. We all know a little booze is good both for the psyche and one's health. A brandy of an evening or a Scotch n' rocks or some chianti with your spaghetti not only tastes good but it revivifies your blood and aids digestion.

If your wife undergoes some bizarre religious experience and adopts a creed which abhors all alcohol and begins berating you with Bible passages and insists booze is the devil's brew, you've got to fight back as suggested before. The principle's the same. The fight isn't over booze but rather your freedom and God-given right to be yourself, to keep your own personality intact. Fight on, amigo, for the stakes are high.

[Incidentally, how do these Christian zealots justify the idea that alcohol is somehow evil and sinful when the Bible is replete with stories of Jesus turning water into wine and passing pitchers of the stuff back and forth at early lunches and last suppers?]

Incredible.

Still, don't forget booze can be pernicious stuff. It gets people by the throat and won't let go. There are few sorrier sights than some poor bastard whose mind's been paralyzed by demon rum. And there's the drunk driving thing, too. Bad business. All in all, it's best to drink with discretion. A few beers, a brandy or two, and let it go. It's not worth all the trouble it causes.

It's a good idea to reinforce your position in the vice area by adding new ones as you go along. The idea is to keep her off balance, throw the old change-up now and again. For example, you may get tired of bowling after a while and drop out of the Tuesday night league. Okay, then you take up, say, the track and go there on Tuesdays instead. Or just add a new vice to your old ones to show her who's in charge. The point is, play hardball.

Remember that you don't have to win every fight as long as you win the big ones. If cracking your knuckles irritates her, stop doing it. It'll make her feel good and assuage her ego a bit. Or stop trimming your moustache and littering the sink with clippings if it pisses her off. You can safely give up clipping your toenails and shooting the nails all over the room if she asks you to. Or agree to put the toilet seat down. These aren't important enough issues to wax wroth over and they can easily be conceded as throwaway skirmishes in the ongoing marital warfare in which you're engaged.

If you play your cards right, you should be able to preserve all your major vices and maybe even add a few more. There's no reason why you shouldn't slide gracefully into old age with a big fat cigar in your mouth and a snifter of brandy in your hand while picking the winners in the day's racing news. Look around. Lots of other guys do it. And how did they manage it? Easy. They followed the rules laid out in this book, that's how.

It's all in the wrist, you know.

SURVIVAL RULES:

1. **Most wives want to change their husbands; it's genetic.**
2. **Watch for early signs and resist them.**
3. **Remember, the best defense is a good offense. Smoke more not less, go out two nights instead of one, etc.**
4. **Drink if she's against it, but watch the booze; it can creep up on you.**
5. **Add new vices from time to time as a show of independence.**

Eighteen

SEX — AN OVERVIEW

Okay, this is the big one. Now that we're warmed up a bit maybe we can tackle the old sex bugaboo and see if we can set you straight on the subject once and for all.

For openers, men and women are different. Oh, I don't mean anatomically. No, I'm talking about how we perceive sex. As I indicated earlier, men and women are psychologically, spiritually, physiologically, emotionally, culturally, and instinctively different in their approach to getting laid. In fact, we're so different it's a wonder anybody ever gets any at all.

Consider the facts. Man has always thought of sex as a lark, a game; we even talk about scoring as though we were playing football or something, but women rarely see it that way and it all has to do with anatomy. Men dally and move on but women are left with the consequences of that dalliance and end up pregnant. While Don Juan is scaling the widow's balcony down the block, his latest conquest is anxiously counting the days since her last period and wondering what she's going to tell her husband who's been out of town for two months.

Since a woman does get pregnant, it's never been to her advantage to casually dispense her favors in a willy-nilly fashion. In fact, it's much better for her if she can trick some joker into agreeing to hang around indefinitely by withholding said favors and using the promise of them to lure him into something resembling matrimony. That way he has to provide sustenance for her and hers and it's an altogether better arrangement for her.

Nor can we fault her for this. If men had the kids we'd hold out for some similar scheme ourselves. It's no fun trying to raise a brood of kids sans help with their care and feeding. Ask any of the millions of modern-day women who are currently doing just that.

So women have regarded getting laid in a different light than men since prehistoric times. This is where all this "commitment" crap comes from. There are still countless women out there who think that giving a guy some must automatically result in a commitment, a term that means you give up your present lifestyle and start living as I want you to. What rubbish in these times!

Anyway, in keeping with this fact, women early on built strategies designed to keep men at arm's length until they'd worked out some form of commitment. They were aided and abetted in this by their mothers who were also women and therefore well aware of the consequences of uncommited dallying. The last thing mother wanted was for daughter to dally and bring the kid home for her to raise, a phenomenon that continues to occur regularly even today.

So girls learned to avoid sex. Their entire education was centered around chastity, virtue, purity, and similar nonsense. But they were also taught that sex was their chief asset as far as getting a husband was concerned, so they learned the skills of flirtation and seduction and deception. Offer much and give as little as possible. Never show 'em a glimpse of thigh when an exposed calf will do the job. Cleavage is good but don't reveal all lest the magic of the thing be lost.

Well, it worked. Set up a society where nobody gets laid until he agrees to the terms of a marriage contract and you'll have husbands all over the place. I mean, given a choice between celibacy and any other alternative, nine guys out of ten will knuckle under and opt for the nooky. Hell, wouldn't you?

Well, while girls are being taught to avoid sex guys are learning to get as much as they possibly can and, that being the case, it's obvious we're going to have an impasse of some kind. And so we have.

Boys instinctively look for action as soon as those dreaded pheromones hit the air and they're encouraged by a society that winks at young men sowing wild oats. After all, they're just being boys, aren't they? It's normal for boys to experiment, to gain experience, to lose their virginity and become men. Hasn't it always been so?

So there you are. The girls are saying no and the boys are beside themselves with unsown oats.

Until now, that is. Nowadays, kids are getting laid at ever younger ages. Over half of 'em couldn't qualify for the role of virgin in the school pageant by the time they're sixteen, and almost none of 'em would be suitable for that role by the time they leave high school.

There are two reasons for this phenomenon. The first is changing moral attitudes about getting laid before somebody's officially sanctioned it. Nobody

gives a damn now, no one disapproves except people with a vested interest in seeing things remain
the same. We no longer label premarital sex as a sin
or wrong or embarrassing. Women today casually
have so-called illegitimate kids and announce their
arrival in the local paper. Teen-agers in their ninth
month unconcernedly parade through the hallways
of their high schools and teachers routinely keep on
hand tubs of boiling water and lots of sheets to tear
up in case of emergency deliveries during class.
Nobody cares any more. You get laid or you don't.
Period.

Then there's birth control. We've so perfected the
art that no one has to get pregnant, and even if she
does she has the choice of abortion to fall back on.
All the rules have been changed; it's a new ball
game, and these changes have radically changed
the marriage game.

Anyway, these earlier attitudes still contribute to
how women deal with sex in spite of recent
changes. The idea of holding out is inbred in 'em
psychologically. Everybody knows it, too. Consider.
Guys lay girls; girls get laid. We score; women get
scored upon. Men are studs; women sluts, tramps.
Don Juan is revered; his conquests reviled. This all
stems from the idea that good women don't do it
while boys will be boys.

Is it any wonder so many of us have been
screwed up for so long?

Incidentally, it's a well-known fact that men like
sex more than women do and... What? Someone (a
woman?) says it isn't so? Ah, but it is, demon-
strably so. Consider the facts.

88

All normal guys are constantly on the lookout for any spare sex they can get. Give the average guy a chance to get laid and he'll take it no questions asked. He won't insist on building a lasting relationship or arranging some kind of exclusivity deal or eating dinner first or any of that crap; he'll just get right down to business and get the thing done.

Most women won't do that. How do I know? Because they don't, that's how. While the average guy will get laid on his lunch hour he usually doesn't because he can't find casual partners who'll accommodate him, but that's not so for women. Any reasonably attractive woman can sidle up to a handsome colleague at work and suggest they "do" lunch in the supply room and bam! she's getting laid just like that.

But when's the last time this happened to you? See? Women can have all the guys they want, where they want, and when they want, and yet most of 'em are clinging tenaciously to one poor sap and bitching because he's oversexed, for God's sake. If they liked sex as much as we do, women would be getting laid in supply rooms, cabs, doorways, elevators, and cloak rooms all hours of the day and night. And so would we, I might add. Ah, just think of it. Unlimited nooky. What guy could ask for more?

So there you have it. Woman can and won't; men will and can't because they won't let us. Who likes it more? I rest my case.

SURVIVAL RULES:

1. Men and women are different because
   a. men think of sex as fun...
   b. ...while women hardly think of it at all.
2. Women will deny the above but it's still true. Ask any guy.

Nineteen

SEX — PICKING
A WINNER

So you're dating this woman and you want to know if she's sexually suitable. You can't tell just by the quality you get before you're married, of course, since she's working full-time at deceiving your ass in every way possible. Many a guy has marched to the altar convinced he's getting a sexual dynamo when he's actually marrying a complete dud.

First of all, she'll start by deceiving you as to her overall experience. To hear her tell it, her hymen broke when she was riding horseback at summer camp when the truth is she sneaked over to the boys' camp and laid everybody in the Indian Guide hut. She claims she lost her virginity at nineteen in a single encounter with a college senior after going with him for two whole years and that's a lot of crap, too.

The truth is, the lady's lost count of 'em. She probably couldn't guess the players within a dozen or so, but she's going to convince you she's practically a virgin and chances are you'll buy it. She pretends to know little in terms of techniques the first few times you make out, but it's astounding how quickly she learns. In no time she's suggesting sexual acrobatics unheard of even in the Kamasutra, for Christ's sake.

91

And is she orgasmic? Are you kidding? Every experience improves on the last one, she's enthusiastic and willing and cries out passionately and leads to you believe a) that you're a fantastic lover and b) she loves sex every bit as much as you do. But does she?

Marry her and find out. All of a sudden — and I mean on the damn honeymoon, pal — she isn't all that crazy about getting laid and tells you so.

"Hey, c'mere, let's get a quickie," you say after lunch on the first day of your honeymoon.

"Oh, wait, I've, uh, got a little headache, honey," she says. "Let's wait till tonight, okay?"

And that's it. Before you know it she's got your ass on a schedule of some kind and that's it for the next forty years. Maybe it's two or three times a week if you're lucky, or maybe once a month whether you're horny or not. It's true. There are actually guys out there who get some as seldom as once a month. They may want it five times a week but they score monthly and that's the end of it.

And it's their own fault, too. If they paid attention before marriage, they might have made a better choice. For instance, those orgasms we mentioned above. How do you know they're real? Do you know that many women fake 'em at regular intervals? If there's a woman out there who's *never* faked an orgasm, she's unknown to medical science. The average woman can make an actress as sharp as Meryl Streep look like the merest beginner when it comes to faking orgasms. You'd swear she's experiencing sexual nirvana and all the time she's planning what she's going to wear tomorrow and wishing you'd hurry up and finish.

92

How can you guard against such deception? You can't. As I said, they're just too good at it. They're so good most of 'em could be hooked to a lie detector and come off looking like paragons of truth every time. But there are some things you can do to get a general idea of her real self.

For example, have a long engagement, a real long one, and during that time get laid as often as possible. Try to drop by every night (except Wednesdays and alternate Fridays, of course) and get some. Sleep over now and then and score in the morning and note whether her enthusiasm changes at dawn. Stay a weekend and aim for six or seven sessions and see if she balks or if the quality falls off from first to last.

See if she's a closet dresser. If she is, beat a hasty retreat. There's no surer sign a woman's got severe sexual hang-ups than if she won't let you see her naked. I mean, if her body's in such bad shape she's ashamed to bare it, why would you want her in the first place? Who wants to be saddled with such a woman?

And don't think her so-called modesty is cute or becoming. She doesn't like sex and nakedness and all the other good stuff associated with these things and you're better off without her. As soon as she ducks into the closet, you duck out the front door and don't look back.

Another test is to see if she ever makes the first move. Women who really like sex will often get turned on spontaneously (as we do!) and start things rolling on their own. Such women are highly prized everywhere, of course, and not available in very large quantities, so if you find one sign her up

94

at once and assure yourself lifelong sexual happiness. You'll be a lucky man, indeed.

There's another gambit you can use to test for sexual integrity. After you've gone with her for six months or so and settled into a pattern, deliberately slack off and see what happens. If you've been getting it five times a week and suddenly cut back to, say, twice a week and she quickly accepts the decrease, watch out. It means she wasn't all that excited about the quantity and will willingly, even gladly, settle for less. In other words, she was faking you out.

Marry such a woman and she'll have you on a twice monthly schedule in no time at all and you'll join that vast army of sexually dissatisfied men flooding the landscape in this and other lands.

Another thing, check out what she reads or watches on TV. If she has copies of Playgirl lying around her place, that's a very good sign. Women who like to look at naked men are the kind you want to know and identify with. It means they'd probably like to see you naked and if that happens they're likely to be naked themselves and that situation could easily lead to still another score.

Check out her bookshelves. Are there lots of books with a religious bent like biographies of Joan of Arc or Mother Teresa or St. Thomas Aquinas' Summa Theologica or The Lives of Famous Nuns, etc? Dump her. She'll surely regard the whole thing as fundamentally immoral and aesthetically messy and you'll end up a reluctant celibate.

On the other hand, if her shelves are crammed with cheap romance novels and well-worn copies of the Kamasutra, you're in luck. It's a good bet she likes sex and that means you'll probably like her.

What does she watch on TV? Does she have cable? The Playboy Channel? Does she like steamy movies with lots of torn bodices and great looking guys giving the heroines what for? How about a VCR? Does she rent X-rated movies, or how does she react when you bring 'em over? Does she willingly reenact 'em with some enthusiasm?

Will she play games like Little Bo Peep or the Door-to-Door Salesman or the Telephone Repairman? Does she favor exotic underwear and offer to model same? Will she let you videotape things? Does she own one or more dildos and do they appear well-worn?

Well, you get the idea. It's all a matter of knowing what to look for and then paying attention. With a little effort on your part, you can easily weed out the sexual losers and guarantee yourself a wife who can still work magic years after you've become an old geezer.

SURVIVAL RULES:
1. **She'll deceive you...**
2. **...and you'll fall for it hook, line, and sinker.**
3. **Be wary of "scheduled" sex — unless you're the one making the schedule.**
4. **Have a long engagement and check her out thoroughly.**

Twenty

AFFAIRS (YOURS)

So now you're married. It's a done deal, the ink is dry on the license and your wife's already filed it away with her attorney. Gone are the halcyon days of irresponsible youth, of laughter and fun weekends and exciting new conquests, and all replaced with domesticity and order and steadiness. Some people call it settling down but a lot of husbands call it other things — all unprintable here.

You're playing with different rules now, you've taken on a partner who's already hard at work turning the arrangement into a sole proprietorship with herself as the lone stockholder. You're what's called a husband, one of an anonymous class of faceless men who toil at uninspiring jobs and dream fondly of pirates and bounding mains and adventure and...

But it's too late for that now. Let's see, where are we? Oh, yes, trying to salvage something of your sex life.

We'll start with affairs. It is, of course, a given that you'll have one or more affairs during your marriage. How do I know? Because everybody does, or nearly everybody. There are guys out there who can't get it up any more or who are so terrorized by their wives they couldn't pull it off with a set of Playboy twins but these guys obviously don't count. The fact is, some seventy or eighty percent of able-bodied American men have affairs during their married life. (So do as many as fifty percent of American wives but that's another story to be told later.)

These aren't my figures; nearly everyone agrees they're accurate. And that brings up an interesting point while we're on the subject. I claim that extramarital sex is not an aberration at all; that it is, in fact, absolutely normal behavior wherever men congregate.

Think about it. What makes something a norm? Why, something everybody does, of course. If the vast majority of the population uses foul language, then swearing could be said to be a norm of the society — and it would be, too. If most people lose their virginity by fifteen, then early loss of virginity would be a norm. So, if, say, seventy-five percent of American men have extramarital affairs, then infidelity is a norm in this society. What could be more obvious?

Not only that, but everybody knows monogamy is completely foreign to man and always has been. The whole concept has been foisted off on us by women who wanted security and somebody of their very own to abuse as well as political leaders who were anxious to attain stability amongst restless and volatile subjects and sought to avoid conflict arising from some guy waltzing another dude's missus.

Under these circumstances, why should men be faithful? And to whom? Should we surrender a basic condition that makes men men in the first place merely because a lot of conniving women selfishly demand it? And a bunch of charlatans and frauds who've managed to inveigle positions of power long for easier control of their subjects?

Well, even if society goes on claiming monogamy is the only right way for men to live, men themselves will give the lie to the theory as long as primal urges and atavistic yearnings are a part of us. No one, not even society or religion or selfish women can stop men from being men in the long run. We can't say no to nature, such a thing isn't possible.

Okay, so we'll start with affairs. Oh, I don't mean you'll have an affair the first week or so but, as we've seen, you'll have 'em eventually so we may as well examine this phenomenon and see what makes it tick.

You say you love your wife and don't plan to have an affair? Well, of course you do! You're only just married, you've still got rice in your pockets and delusions in your head; of course you still love your new bride and you always will, too. Still...

See, things happen, as they say. Let's suppose you followed all the rules outlined in previous chapters and really 'scoped this woman out thoroughly before marriage and managed to pick a winner. Even so, sooner or later some sloe-eyed little vixen down at the office will look at you over her computer screen and wink and lust will rear its head and wink back and presto! you're involved in an affair.

Now, let's analyze this situation. Does this mean there's something wrong with your marriage? Not necessarily, though it's likely since there's something wrong in nearly every marriage. The chances are you're a little bored and the passion has long since fizzled out. Maybe your wife refuses to be Bo

Peep any more, or she's gained fifty pounds and lost some of her appeal, or she's a nag and a shrew and a real drag, so the sloe-eyed vixen looks pretty good to you about now.

On the other hand, though, your marriage may be in fine fettle and entirely without major problems, but the vixen will tempt you anyway. Why is this so? Because she represents variety, something new and different, something exciting, maybe even dangerous, and you, a would-be pirate and sailor of bounding mains, long for the chase again. Clandestine meetings, forbidden fruit, wild, tempestuous sex in strange surroundings with exotic sloe-eyed vixens. Egad! What real man could resist such a challenge?

But wait. You've made vows, haven't you? Sacred ones in a church filled with witnesses and you're a man of honor, are you not? Certainly you are. But what about those vows? I mean, are they strictly binding in a legal sense? Maybe not. Consider. The courts say one may not be coerced into a contract, that one must voluntarily agree to its terms or it won't be legal.

Well, what about your vows? If that wasn't a case of blind coercion, I've never seen one before. Here you are a poor sap overcome with this strange malady called love and entirely bereft of your judgment and dazzled by promises of unimaginable bliss, and then you're asked to swear lifetime faithfulness to a woman you hardly know while hundreds of spectators look on. You don't think that's coercion?!

Suppose you had second thoughts at the very moment the preacher is running that "forsaking all others" crap by you. What man could renege then? Right, you go ahead and lock yourself in. You are coerced.

Besides, think how irrational it all is. How can any man reasonably promise that any given woman will be able to meet all his needs for eternity? Impossible. Note how many divorces there are and you'll agree such promises are on mighty shaky ground.

Well, now that you've disposed of the legal and moral niceties, you decide to throw caution to the wind and go for it. As someone once said, live dangerously for it's the only time you live at all. Isn't it about time you lived a little?

Okay, back to Miss Sloe-eyed. Your first concern is your intended paramour. Who is she? What's her angle? Is she married? These are vital questions since the outcome of the affair will depend on just such considerations.

Take the married question. Married women make for better and more successful affairs than single women, especially if she's more or less happily married. Such a woman is probably just looking for some relief from the boredom brought on by living with her dull clod of a husband who probably never even heard of Little Bo Peep. She doesn't want out of her marriage, she just wants a little fun.

Good. That means no complications, no crazy talk of commitment. She won't be haranguing you after the second liaison to leave your wife and run away with her.

But beware if she's unhappily married and looking for a new sap to replace her present one. Such women are utterly without scruples and will go to any length to ruin your marriage in hopes of snaring you themselves. You must tread cautiously at first to ascertain her motives.

After that first glimpse over the computer screen and a few well-directed meaningful glances, you'll agree to rendezvous for a drink after work and size each other up, as it were. Okay. Choose a discreet place, some dimly lit watering spa across town which is unlikely to attract any of your acquaintances. Take a booth in the back, one near a rear exit in case you have to beat a hasty retreat.

Once settled, sound her out. Instead of aimless small talk, you want to ask probing questions, questions designed to see where she's coming from. And there's no need to beat around the bush and run the risk of getting ambiguous impressions. For example, this initial conversation might go something like this:

"So, tell me, is your husband a gun fancier?" you ask.

"My husband?" she says laughing. "He wouldn't have a gun in the house. He thinks guns should be outlawed."

See how it goes? Already you've uncovered valuable information, information so valuable it could easily save your worthless hide in the ensuing weeks and months.

But suppose she told you he was a charter member of the National Rifle Assn. and a crack shot who routinely hunted Cape buffalo with a single-shot .22? Drop her on the spot. I'm serious. A guy like that is a public menace who'll riddle your ass with buckshot if he gets wind that you're laying his wife. Tell her straight out you're not interested and head for the door. No woman is worth such a risk, I don't give a damn how sloe-eyed she is.

But we're going with the first answer here so you press on. "I'll bet he's some enormous guy who played linebacker for the Rams, then, eh?" you say.

"No, Freddie's half your size," she responds. "He hates violence of any kind. In fact, he's a Quaker and violence is against his religion. He thinks all troubles can be solved intellectually and peacefully."

Now you're cooking! First, he's Freddie in the diminutive and that's a good sign. Guys called Freddie and Jimmy and Tommy are a lot less likely to be overly aggressive than guys named Joe or Jake or Ox. And then he's a little guy only half your size. Why, if he shows up unexpectedly, you can knock him on his ass and you're in the clear.

Follow up with questions aimed at learning her domestic situation.

"Sounds like a sensible guy," you say. "You're lucky. There are a lot of losers out there."

"Yeah, I guess I am. We hardly ever fight or anything, it's just that, well, you know, sometimes it's a little, well, boring, I guess..."

Well, is this one perfect or what? Happily married to a wimpy husband and out to put a little spark in her life. What more could you ask for?

All right, now let's look at single women for a minute. Affairs with them are okay but they just pose more problems than married ones. A major concern is so many of the scheming hussies are vicious manhunters who deliberately set their caps for any bozo who happens by with an eye to nailing his ass in marriage.

This type looks for a chance to let your wife know what's going on because she hopes to gain when your current marriage falls apart, so she'll pull capers like calling and hanging up to raise her suspicions, or calling and asking for you knowing you'll be hard pressed to explain who the hell she is and why she's calling you. Sooner or later she'll show up on your porch in order to confront your wife and demand that she give you up, etc.

She'll make sure there's lipstick on your collar after every assignation. She'll leave earrings in your coat pocket, lipstick-covered kleenex in your car, long blond hairs all over the place, surreptitiously soak your suits with perfume, send birthday cards to your house, and bedevil your ass in a hundred other ways until you regret the day the bitch first peered at you over that computer screen.

Another reason single women aren't good prospects for affairs is because they want more of your time than you care to give. They want you to stay overnight, for example, when that's impossible and they know it. Or they'll want romantic week-ends which are equally impossible. They also expect gifts, and the more expensive the better. (Married women never want gifts because they'd have to explain 'em to their suspicious husbands.)

And single women are more likely to turn up pregnant and name your ass as the father and you could end up in a paternity suit and have to pay support for the next eighteen years, for Christ's sake. Naturally, they'll refuse to get an abortion since abortion is against their religion. And isn't it funny how these types never seem to worry about religion while they're busy re-enacting Debbie doing Dallas?

Astonishing.

(Incidentally, married women can't pull this pregnancy dodge since the law assumes any offspring are automatically their husbands'.)

All right, so you've analyzed Miss Sloe-eyed and know her to be a happily married woman who's wimpy husband is a pacifist. She only wants a little excitement to add some zest and sparkle to her otherwise drab existence. Perfect.

So you've had your first tentative meetings and are now ready for action. All that remains is to find a convenient motel with low rates and get the show on the road. You'll want to practice safe sex, of course, especially if this is an affair of the one-night stand variety since women who go in for these spontaneous liaisons generally have a lot of 'em and thereby increase their chances of having contracted some nightmarish disease. The married lady at the next computer terminal is less likely to be quite so cavalier about her escapades and is thereby a safer commodity overall.

And now let me show you the advantages of planning ahead. Remember those earlier warnings about nights out? Remember your Wednesdays and alternate Fridays? Well, now you see one of the reasons for setting 'em up.

Let's face it, one of the biggest problems in carrying on an affair is finding the time to do it. You have to be able to account for blocks of time spent laying your paramour in that cheap motel and that's not easy to do unless you're married to a woman with an IQ below eighty or one who's busy laying the guy across the street and doesn't have time to worry about you.

Look, suppose you've been married for ten years and during that time you never set up a regular night out. Maybe you're almost never out at night without the little woman tagging along. Okay. So Miss Sloe-eyed vamps your ass at work and you long to give her what for in the worst way. You approach her and ... what?

Ask her out for a drink? What'll you tell your wife, pal? You haven't missed the 5:20 commuter in ten years and all of a sudden you don't show up till 8:40. Where were you? Why didn't you call? What's going on here? Etc.

Is she a bitch? Certainly not. Under the circumstances, these are reasonable questions. You vary your routine for the first time in a decade and you're surprised she asks questions about it? Even a slow-witted woman would be curious, wouldn't she? Think, man, think. You'll never last a day in the world of illicit love if you aren't ever on your guard.

But you don't have that worry since you planned ahead at the very start and arranged free time in abundance. All you have to do is tell Miss Sloe-eyed that Wednesday is fine with you and you're in business because the missus never expects to see your ass on Wednesday. It's bowling night, remember? You meet some bowling buddies for dinner and then repair to the alley and bowl until nine and then some of the boys stop by Al's house and have a few drinks and you've covered your ass from five o'clock until midnight and never a suspicion raised.

Isn't that beautiful?

Those Fridays come in handy, too. Lots of times, especially if you're consorting with a single woman, it's convenient to have a weekend spot available for romantic trysts during the peak social hours and you're all set because Fridays are poker night. They're also late nights since you had the good sense to get home very late from many of those outings, so late that three a.m. would cause no unnecessary concern on the home front.

While your married buddies were letting themselves be molded like so many plugs of silly putty, you were laying the groundwork for a future you'd have some say in and now it's paid off.

And another thing. Remember my advice to handle the money? Do you see one of the pluses of that now? Affairs cost money, you know. We still live in a sick society where the man is expected to pay for everything while the woman merely provides her precious self. And as long as this grossly unfair standard persists, it'll be up to you to pay for the room, buy dinner, pick up bar tabs, and so on. You'll need money.

Now, if you've foolishly let your wife handle the money and she's been giving you an allowance of, say, thirty bucks a week for lunches, parking, and whatnot, and that's all you've been getting for the last ten years since you never leave the house alone and thus have no personal expenses, how the hell do you plan to come up with the necessary cash to cover those motel rooms?

"Uh, say, honey, uh, could I have, uh, fifty dollars for, uh, something I need and, uh..." you say.

107

And what does she say? "Fifty bucks?! What the hell do you need fifty bucks for? What the hell's goin' on around here, buddy? You're up to something, aren't you?" Etc., etc.

Not a chance. Even if you came up with a plausible story for the first fifty, even the dullest of women would start adding things up when you came back the third or fourth time and it'd be all over.

But since you followed my advice and took charge of the money yourself, there's no problem at all. The missus doesn't have the foggiest idea of your finances since you never tell her anything. You need a fast fifty, you write a check on your account confident that she'll never sort through the cancelled checks to find you out. Or pay for the room with VISA since she doesn't pay the bills and will never see it. What could be easier?

And don't forget that private account you've squirreled away for yourself over the years. If you've been stashing away imaginary poker losses and bowling league dues right along, there should be a substantial sum by this time, enough to more than handle a first-rate affair and leave some for the next one.

There, aren't you glad you read this book?

Okay, so are there danger signs once you've launched the affair? Damn right there are, and the biggest one is when she says anything at all about love. If she lets fall a single word to the effect that she loves you, she's history. Assume a shocked look, get dressed, and get out. It's a sure sign you've misjudged her, she's a schemer who won't be satisfied until she's completely ruined your life and driven you to despair.

Remember, you only want an affair, a little fun. You've already got a wife and don't need another one. This love talk will end badly every time; the next thing you know she'll be talking about commitment. Lose her.

Once started, how long will it run? Usually, not too long; that's why they call 'em affairs. A few weeks, a couple of months or so, and it's over. How do you break it off? Easy. Stop asking her out. When she asks you, be busy. Claim things are rocky at home just now and you have to ease up a bit. Say you think your wife suspects something. She'll get the idea. It won't be as traumatic as you might think, especially if you've chosen carefully. After all, she was only in it for the fun herself and didn't want any complications, either. She'll probably be just as glad it's over and would have ended it herself in another week or so.

When you do stop, though, have a little class. Make an effort to keep her friendship. Go out now and then for a drink. Stop and chat at the water cooler. Ask her how she's doing, how things are with Freddie, give her a wink now and again. If it was something you both enjoyed, why shouldn't you both have good memories to take away with you?

As I said, have a little class.

SURVIVAL RULES:

1. Everybody has affairs; it's a social norm everywhere.
2. Lay plans for future lays early.
3. Choose married paramours over single, ones with pacifist husbands weighing forty or so pounds less than you do.
4. Keep a clear conscience. Remember, those so-called sacred vows are meaningless because you were tricked.
5. Never tell them you love 'em. You'll regret it if you do.
6. Go out with class. Keep the friendship when it's over.

Twenty-One

AFFAIRS (YOUR WIFE'S)

Now, what about her affairs? Alas, it's true, there are always two sides to every coin. We commented earlier that just as seventy or more percent of American husbands have extramarital affairs, so do fifty percent of American wives. Oh, it's shocking, all right, it's a terrible indictment of the perfidy of American womanhood, but it's the God's honest truth and we have to face up to it.

This means that for every two of you guys out there who are reading these words, one of your wives is getting laid regularly and adorning you with the cuckold's horns in the process. Geez, doesn't the mere thought of it piss you off, though?

What makes 'em do it? Have they no respect for their sacred vows to "love, honor, and obey" your ass till death do you part? Is laying the neighbors any way to show love and honor, for Christ's sake? Has she no scruples, no integrity, no consideration?

(What's that? You say I'm wrong in holding her to her vows while excusing the guy from his on the grounds that he was coerced? Well, I'm consistent if nothing else so I've got that covered. She *wasn't* coerced; in fact, she and her conniving mother were the coerceors and that means she can be held accountable and he can't. Isn't that simple?)

It's different when a guy plays around because everybody knows that's what guys do, but a guy's wife is expected to do right and conduct herself as a lady at all times. If she's the town slut she'll bring dishonor to her husband and no real man can tolerate that in any society, ergo, she mustn't play around.

Okay, how do you know if she is? Well, by some of the same ways she'd know if you were. Take the time element. If she goes to aerobics every Wednesday and visits with her sorority sisters every other Friday, you may already be in deep trouble. If she's got that much unrestricted time, she could lay whole bowling teams and you'd never be the wiser.

The mistake here is in allowing her those nights out in the first place. Remember, this is your wife we're talking about, your woman. How would it look to your friends if your wife were regularly seen coming home late (three a.m.!)? What would people think? They'd think she was out playing around on your ass, that's what they'd think.

In no time you'd be known as the neighborhood cuckold. You wouldn't be able to walk past the pool hall and look the guys in the eye, especially since some of 'em are probably the ones laying your wife. Their laughter and jibes would ring in your ears as you passed and you'd be humiliated beyond belief.

Outrageous.

Well, how are you to avoid such a scene? Easy. Don't let her get away with it, that's how. And you can start by not letting her out alone at night. When the issue first arises, tell her it's a cultural thing with Kurds that their women are not allowed to go out on the town by themselves. If she won't buy this, or refuses to believe you're a Kurd, insist that she not be out later than, say, eight-thirty, and that she is only allowed in public places like malls and crowded restaurants as you're worried about her safety what with the high crime rate and all. She might buy this because it looks like you're only concerned about her well-being and are just being a dutiful husband.

So limiting her free time is a good first step. As you know from personal experience, affairs take time and if she hasn't got any to spare she's less likely to screw around on you. But is eight-thirty going to help? A resourceful woman could seduce three or four guys in an hour or so if she put her mind — and other resources — to it, couldn't she?

Sure, she could, but we aren't done yet. Making her punch a clock is only one arrow in our anti-cuckold quiver. There are lots of old stand-bys suspicious husbands have used for centuries, tricks so good they've stood the test of time and have been passed down to us today. Why, ancient Romans used the old come-home-early trick and waylaid wayward wives.

It's simplicity itself. What you do is claim you've got to go out of town for a few days. If you already travel in your job it's a snap, but even if you don't you can set up a weekend fishing trip with the boys and still make it work. Be sure to give her plenty of notice so she'll have time to arrange a tryst with the guy and then take off.

If you've made it a weekend, it gives you an entire Friday night to cut loose on your own and even Saturday day, but Saturday night you head home a whole day early and spring the trap. It's a good idea to call her sometime Saturday evening to assure her you're still up in the woods or in Cleve-

113

land or wherever, and tell her you'll see her Sunday night as planned. Around eleven or so you hit the front door and make a beeline for the bedroom and catch her in the damn act, by God!

Okay, so far so good, but now what? You've got 'em dead to rights, and by rights they should be dead, but what exactly do you do? I mean, do you shoot 'em? Grab the guy and punch his head off? Or punch *her* head off? Sit down and discuss the situation rationally like so-called civilized people? Throw both of 'em out?

It's important you think this out early on so you won't do anything rash and live to regret it. I knew one guy, for example, who's best friend was laying his wife and the poor sap was a laughingstock in the local pool hall. Well, one day he used the come-home-early ruse and caught 'em in flagrante delicto, went nuts, grabbed a gun and shot the guy in the leg. He was arrested and sent to the big house for three-to-five years and his buddy moved in with his missus. Now he's a laughingstock in every pool hall for miles around — and in the state pen, too!

Well, learn from his mistake. You want to fix her wagon for adorning your brow with horns and make sure she doesn't do it again, and you also want to fix lover boy's ass so he knows he's dealing with a real man here, by God. So grab your kid's authentic-looking Uzi and put it on 'em. (Be sure the damn thing isn't real, though; you don't want any accidents.) Order 'em out of bed and threaten to shoot both of 'em on the spot. Scare 'em good. Act wild, deranged. Do it right and this dude won't even be able to get it up for the next six months.

Then throw the guy out. Tell him if he ever shows his mug around your wife again you'll drill his ass full of holes like a Swiss cheese. Tell your wife the same thing; let her know you're no fool. Ground her for six months or so. Cut up her credit cards for a whole year. Refuse to let her mother in the house for two whole years. Tell her you're going to write to Ann Landers and report her ass. In other words, make it a memorable occasion, one she won't easily or soon forget. There's a good chance the woman will never be unfaithful again and you'll have renewed standing in pool halls everywhere.

In some cases you may want to use a variation on the come-home-early caper where you ring the doorbell and then run around back and see who comes out the back door. It fits certain situations better than the former caper. And another variation is where you just hide in the closet and never actually go anywhere. Whatever, the goal's the same.

If she's too clever to go for these tricks, more drastic action may be called for. I mean, suppose she's got some dude at work and she sees him during the day or right after work at night? What then? You hire a private detective, that's what. Look in the yellow pages under gumshoes and sign somebody up. Tell him you want her followed. The guy gets on her trail and if she's playing around, he'll have the goods on her ass in no time and you can fix her wagon for her.

The only problem with this idea is it can be expensive. Private detectives don't come cheap but they're worth it when you consider the stakes. After all, how much is your honor worth to you?

Or you can be your own private detective. When she goes out to meet the girls, you follow her. It's easy. Just like in the movies. When she pulls into L'Affaire Lounge parking lot and gets into some guy's car and heads for the nearby One Nighter Motel, you've got her in the act and can proceed to straighten her out and regain your honor.

You can check her odometer, too. Suppose she says she's just going to the mall and back but you think she's getting some on the side. Okay. Check the odometer before she leaves and look at it again when she gets back. If the mall's ten miles round trip and you see she's driven over forty miles, something's not kosher. Next time you follow her and catch her red-handed.

Still playing detective, what about those mysterious wrong numbers you get by the dozen every week? You know, the ones where the phone rings and you answer it and they hang up. A few minutes later it rings again and she answers it and it's one of her girlfriends. Suspicious? Damn right it is. Well, get yourself one of those new-fangled gadgets that record incoming phone numbers and see if those wrong numbers stop all of a sudden. If they do, you can bet your ass she's getting some on the side and the guys at the pool hall are having a good laugh at your expense.

Watch it, though. If you get one of those gadgets it may work against you. Remember, it'll also record your number when you call from *her* house to say you're working overtime. It's a kind of two-edged sword and may do you more harm than good in the end.

We're still not through, though. One sure-fire way to know there's something funny going on is when your wife comes up with totally new techniques you know damn well she didn't learn from you. I mean, if you're getting laid and she suggests trying the Himalayan Wooden Balls trick and even produces a set of well-worn balls, you've got a problem. Where the hell would she learn something like that?

Or maybe you've been a basic missionary position guy for the last ten years and suddenly she insists on the Satrap's Side Saddle position. It may even be something minor, some slight variation from the norm, or even talking where she never talked before, and you'll know something's up and can take appropriate action.

Finally, you can always resort to technology. There are stores now that sell all kinds of bugging devices. They've got miniature camcorders you hide in flower pots or behind the sugar bowl, tape recorders, phone bugs, electronic eavesdropping gadgets that let you hear clearly from a thousand yards, voice-activated stuff that even saves on batteries, and hundreds of other items that'll let you spy on her ass twenty-four hours a day. If she makes a single wrong move, bam! you'll have her in your sights, by God!

So there you have it. A wayward wife can be a pain in the ass and make a man look bad to his peers, but these suggestions can go a long way to either prevent her from straying in the first place or catch her at it if she does. It is, after all, a matter of honor, of manhood, of pride, and your reputation with pool hall habitues everywhere.

SURVIVAL RULES:

1. You can't trust them; most women have no scruples.
2. An affair is a different matter when it's your wife who's playing around.
3. Set the rules early; let her know Kurds don't tolerate any funny stuff, by God.
4. Watch for signs. You'll know them when you see 'em since they're the same ones you pull on her.
5. Remember, your honor's at stake: the guys at the pool hall are watching you.

Twenty-Two

SEX — ADDING SPICE

Okay, so we've dealt with the major aspects of this sex business and got some insight into what makes the whole thing work. But there are some other points we should consider which are sex-related and therefore important.

Maintaining a good sex life can be hard to do, especially if you ended up with a religious freak or basic prude through some miscalculation or other, but there are some things you can do that'll help.

If your wife'll cooperate, you can videotape things and pretend you're filming porno flicks with Marilyn Chambers or guiding Debbie through Dallas and thereby provide another element in an otherwise boring sex life. Just be sure you remove the tape if you rent the camcorder. I've heard of a number of cases where somebody forgot and took it back to the video store and the damn tape showed up on the evening news.

Again, drag out the Little Bo Peep costumes. It's estimated that the vast majority of American couples play games of one kind or another in the bedroom and why not? Let's face it, after ten or twenty years of the same thing anything'd get dull. If you can do something to spice things up, so much the better.

Some couples get turned on by getting laid in places where there's a high risk of being caught. These people make out in elevators and airplanes, behind potted palms, on park benches and what have you. This requires a wife with a certain temperament, of course, but it's worth running it up the old flag pole. Who knows, maybe she'll salute it.

As mentioned earlier, X-rated videos can be a turn on. If they work for you, you should have a well-stocked library for emergency use and save untold trips to the video store. Or send your wife to one of those sexy lingerie stores where she can load up on edible panties and pop up bras and see-through nighties and garter belts and all the rest.

Dildos are good, big ugly ones with huge warts and bumps all over 'em. Lots of women seem to like these things and they can help a lot, but be careful she doesn't end up getting more fun out of the dildo than she does you. Many a husband has learned to his sorrow that a fat, foot-long dildo can make his own four-incher look pretty inadequate indeed.

Leave the window shades up and the lights on if exhibitionism appeals to you, and that may help. You can even parade around in the buff in front of the lighted windows and help turn on your voyeuristic neighbors and thereby add some spice to *their* sex lives. (Now that's my idea of a good neighbor!)

Order in a supply of cooking oil and some rubber sheets. Invite in some friends. Hire some pretty Oriental masseuses for the evening. Play Sinatra records. Install ceiling mirrors. Rig up swing sets. Buy some whips and chains and ropes. In other words, be imaginative, creative, enterprising. Everything goes nowadays; there are no rules. As they say, whatever turns you on.

All of the above presupposes, of course, a wife who still has something left of her old self. If you don't have one like that, I'm afraid you're out of luck, pal.

SURVIVAL RULES:

1. **Add spice to your marriage. Be creative.**
2. **Beware of extra-large dildos.**

Twenty-Three

SEX — CAVEATS

Since we've seen that women don't like sex as much as we do, we've got to watch out for games they'll play to avoid fulfilling their clearly spelled out duties as specified in the marriage ceremony. Don't forget, the marriage license entitles you to unlimited amounts of sex any time you want it in spite of your wife's claims that it isn't so. Point it out to her. It plainly says "according to the covenants of this document, the husband shall have full conjugal rights at all times..." See?

Well, naturally, she'll try to get out of it. Let me warn you now about one of the most insidious, odious, and outright evil practices ever to come from the mind of woman. Beware of saltpeter!

Ah, you remember that stuff from your army days, eh? It's a chemical that can make men impotent and it's truly barbaric. In fact, there's serious talk of having it banned as uncivilized chemical warfare by the Geneva Convention people. If there was ever a more treacherous substance in man's history, I've never heard of it.

The army used to put it in the food so guys wouldn't get horny and go around collaborating with all the native girls and the damn stuff worked. Some guys still couldn't get it up six months after the damn war was over. Well, I know that there are recorded cases where wives put the stuff in their husbands' food!

It's true. Even your wife might do it. A few sprinkles of the stuff in your scrambled eggs or pea soup and you'll never get it up again until the stuff wears off. If you notice a sudden falling off in interest, search the cupboards. Sneak some mashed potatoes away and have them analyzed by a reliable chemist. Peek around the corner as she fixes the meatloaf and see if she dumps in any mysterious powders.

And if you find out she *has* been feeding you saltpeter, dump her without delay. A woman who'd do such a thing is beyond all salvation and wouldn't profit from a second chance.

Also, beware of mind games designed to undermine your virility. Your wife may deliberately work to destroy your libido by making you feel inadequate. For example, she could make belittling remarks about your dimensions and hint it's not nearly big enough. When she watches porno flicks she'll comment on the hero's size which is at least three times the size of your own and oooh and aaah and generally indicate she'd like to have a go at a real one some day, etc.

Or she'll suggest you read articles lauding the advantages of penile implants to increase size and staying power. Ads extolling various creams and ointments and mechanical gadgets aimed at penile enlargement will be left lying around for you to see. Open copies of Playgirl featuring handsome guys with sausage-like parts will be casually left on the coffee table.

Or she'll tell you in great detail how her friend's husband is a premature ejaculator and how he's been to see the best doctors and the poor woman's going crazy with frustration and what a tragedy it is and so on. She'll follow up with long, languishing silences and heavy sighs every time you have sex and imply that it was less than she might have liked.

Hell, enough of this and you begin to have real doubts about your virility. Once uncertainty sets in, you'll begin to fear the next encounter lest you fail in some way. Apprehension mounts. Next thing you know, you can't get the damn thing up and you're dealing with a full-blown case of impotence and spending a fortune on sex therapists and assorted nostrums and all because the devious bitch has subtly worked you over.

Be on the alert for such shenanigans and nip 'em in the damn bud. Refuse to listen to such crap. If she even hints at such things, assume a righteous air and remind her that you were nationally renowned in the sex department prior to marriage and offered an unconditional guarantee to one and all and never had a single complaint.

In fact, it's a good idea to counterattack at once and suggest that any such failing is likely to be hers. What the hell, let her begin to harbor her own inadequacies.

Okay, that should take care of this sex business. The whole point is, it's largely up to you. Instead of sitting back and letting fate decide what you get, take control of your own destiny and try to rig things to your benefit. Smart guys have always done so, and the rest leave it up to the gods and their wives with predictable results.

SURVIVAL RULES:

1. Beware of mind games!
2. Be even more watchful for signs of saltpeter in your diet.

Twenty-Four

COUNSELING — IF YOU MUST

Sooner or later she'll catch on to your philandering or tire of doing all the housework by herself or whatever, and you'll end up in counseling. All marriages eventually go that route if only because it's chic and very "in" and gives the missus something to talk about at the hairdresser's.

Now, if you've only been married, say, six months and your wife suggests counseling (it's always the wife who suggests counseling), you might want to skip it and write the whole thing off as one of your bigger screw ups. I mean, if things have gone to pot that fast, you both probably need a fresh start.

But if you've been married ten or fifteen years or so, it's a shame to throw all that time away. After that long you've probably got her pretty much the way you want her or you wouldn't — or shouldn't, anyway — still be around. You'd just have to break a new one in and you already know what a job that is, so give counseling a shot.

This is another place where you've got to give the gods a hand before your wife gives you the finger, though. When your wife brings up counseling, and you agree to go, the odds are eight to one she'll offer to set up an appointment — and the same odds say her husband'll let her do it. And that's a mistake.

Guess what sex the counselor will be? You bet your ass she'll be a she. So what, you say? Are you kidding? These lady counselors are usually liberals and feminists, they're Unitarians and Ms. Magazine subscribers, equal-pay-for-equal-work fighters and protest marchers. What chance in hell is there she'll give a damn about anything you have to say? She'll take one look at your chauvinistic ass, cluck disapprovingly and ask your wife to tell her side of the story. They'll never get around to yours, pal.

No, what you want is a guy, preferably one named Tony with a beard and maybe the letters LOVE tatooed across his knuckles. He should wear sweaters and smoke cigars and be macho as hell and have been married at least as long as you have so he'll be sure to understand exactly where you're coming from.

He should *not* be divorced. I don't believe in marriage counselors who've been divorced four or five times. How the hell can he tell me anything when he apparently couldn't handle his own damn wife? And he shouldn't be one of those confirmed never-married bachelors, either. You want a guy with experience in the trenches, a battle-scarred veteran of connubial bliss who knows what it's like to be blissed out and can relate to a fellow sufferer.

You understand, of course, that this counseling business hasn't taken you completely by surprise. After all, you might have suspected you'd end up in counseling when your wife showed you the private detective's report and hopefully you had the good sense to plan ahead.

So when she offers to set up an appointment, you counteroffer. Tell her a guy down at work is in counseling and he suggested one who's top-notch in the field and highly successful. Don't tell her it's a guy unless asked directly. Even then, say it's Dr. So-and-so without using a first name. If she presses further, say you don't know if it's a man or a woman since your friend never said. Besides, you say, what difference would it make? These people are all professionals and they've taken an oath to be unbiased and they'd never let their gender influence 'em and so on. She'll be on the ropes by this time and you can go ahead and set up that appointment with Tony.

You both know the counselor's sex does matter since nobody can ever completely divorce himself from who and what he is, but because you anticipated her you've been able to work it so it looks like she's being contrary and stubborn if she insists on a woman counselor. If it doesn't matter, and she's agreed it doesn't, why wouldn't she accept a male counselor? See? It's just a matter of staying one step ahead of the old bat.

All right, you're at your first session and you're still planning ahead. Relax. Give Tony a good, firm handshake and a nice, manly grin. Don't say much. Let your wife talk — and she will! Women love this kind of stuff. She's got a real, live person who's leaning on her every word and nodding sympathetically and actually listening to her. Sure, the guy's being paid to listen and it's all an act on his part to justify a fee, but she doesn't care. She'll pour forth like Niagara and fill the air with wild tales of how you've abused her and she never gets any cooperation and you hate her mother and she's given you the best years of her life and all that crap. You just sit quietly by and look manly.

Naturally, she comes off looking like a hysterical woman who's probably on a PMS trip or something while you're the very model of reason and calm. By the time she gets done ranting and raving and you get to talk, the counselor will already be shaping his final report in his mind.

You agree that your wife's been harried lately and that you'll do anything to help her pull herself together. Readily admit that you shouldn't have brought Miss Sloe-eyed to your home while your wife was away and that you regret it in the extreme. (This part will be the truth, anyway.) Hint that your wife showed a stinging lack of trust by sneaking back home early and imply it smacks of entrapment, but end by graciously agreeing to accept full responsibility for the whole affair.

By the time your wife catches on to what's going down and tries to recoup, it'll be too late. The rest is just a formality. A few more sessions like the first one and it's all over. Tony will write out a report exonerating you entirely and fixing all the blame on your wife, and she'll be so confused and screwed up she'll no longer be sure what the hell's going on.

From then on you whip out the counselor's report whenever things flare up and hit her with it. Leave copies lying around and highlight the good parts with magic marker. See that her mother gets a copy. Offer to go back for another session with Tony any time she feels the need. Play the supportive husband to the hilt; after all, didn't you get counseling just as she wanted you to? What more could any wife ask?

What, indeed?

Remarkable.

SURVIVAL RULES:

1. Agree to counseling at once if suggested.
2. You pick the counselor, and make it Tony.
3. Let your wife do all the talking.
4. Appear sincere, offer to help her get a grip on herself.
5. Use the counselor's report against her in future disputes.
6. Agree to go back for another session any time.

Twenty-Five

YOUR PRIVACY

The mail arrives and there's a letter addressed to you in a feminine hand. A vague trace of perfume emanates from the envelope. Your wife will not open and read that letter. True or false?

You bet your ass it's false. She'll have that baby steamed open before the sound of the retreating mailman's footsteps fade from the still air. She'll read every word contained therein, dust it for fingerprints, and forward it to a lab for scientific analysis. She'll have it stamped and notarized and registered with the bar association as evidence in any upcoming trial.

In other words, she'll ride roughshod over your constitutional rights to privacy and freedom from illegal search and all the rest of it with never a guilty thought to slow her down. Wives will — and do. Of course, they never admit it since they know full well such behavior is in unthinkably bad taste and indicates a total lack of character and it'd embarrass 'em to be found out, but sneak and pry and snoop they will, regardless.

The thing is, they're insecure and convinced you're on the verge of leaving 'em for another woman or hoarding money on 'em or whatever and they're determined to find out what your game is. So they snoop. You leave your wallet on the dresser while you mow the lawn and she goes through it with a jeweler's loupe looking for phone numbers or bank deposit slips or hotel receipts or anything incriminating she can scare up.

You don't believe me? You say your wife'd never stoop to such unsavory acts? Okay, booby-trap your wallet one time and see. Arrange things in a certain way and see if they've been rearranged in your absence. Put your credit cards, driver's license, and whatnot in some sort of pattern and note whether they've been changed. Put a light piece of thread around your wallet and see if it's broken. Dust your things with that phosphorescent powder stuff and casually flash one of those special lights on her and see if her hands turn purple. You'll be amazed.

What to do about this? Nothing. There's nothing you can do since you can't watch her devious ass twenty-four hours a day, but it's enough if you know it's going on and conduct yourself accordingly.

Get one of those electronic notetaker gadgets, the kind where the user has an entry code and nobody can read it without knowing the code, and keep all your incriminating phone numbers, memos, trysts, etc., in it. Never resort to matchbook covers or cocktail napkins as these items wouldn't get past your wife if she had vision like Ray Charles.

Never have mail sent to your house you don't want her to see. Or a package you don't want her to open. Never get phone calls you don't want her to eavesdrop on. Fit your desk with the finest unpickable locks and hook up an alarm with the Pinkerton people. Remember, you're living with a creature whose curiosity makes a cat's look like complete indifference.

Well, what about her privacy? Does she have any? Sure, she does. You're a gentleman, aren't you? You believe in the Constitution and the concept of unassailable personal rights and fair play, don't you? Of course you do. You have integrity and honor and good breeding and would never invade another's privacy.

Unless you had to, that is.

SURVIVAL RULES:

1. **Most wives snoop.**
2. **Booby trap things to catch her out.**
3. **Secure your stuff with locks, alarms, etc.**
4. **Avoid incriminating mail, phone calls, packages, etc.**
5. **Respect her privacy — unless you have good reason to suspect her.**

Twenty-Six

THE PMS RUSE

Here's another popular ruse wives pull on unsuspecting guys, and it's one that was just invented a few years ago. It's true, PMS was unheard of as recently as 1985. You can research the medical literature before that year and never find a single mention of any woman ever suffering from something called premenstrual syndrome.

Rumor has it that PMS was invented by a Dr. Jose Shapiro, an ob/gyn from Topeka, Kansas. He even wrote a book on the subject called "PMS and American Womanhood" and he went on talk shows everywhere and told women what was wrong with 'em. Naturally, they took to it like a duck to water since it was such an ideal ailment.

I mean, it involves nothing they haven't always had since it only has to do with their monthly visits from the curse fairy. It's not something new that'll kill 'em any time soon, or cause 'em any more inconvenience than they've had right along, but it's a perfect excuse to cover a multitude of sins from just being out of sorts to robbing banks and knocking off unwanted husbands.

It's true. If a woman wants out of a particularly dirty job at the office, she comes down with PMS. If she's late for work, it's not her fault; she's got PMS, that's all. If she doesn't feel like cooking dinner because she's tired from an afternoon of mahjong, she blames it on the ever-reliable PMS. And it's a wonderful cop-out if she doesn't want to give you any within ten or twelve days on either side of her period. "Not tonight, honey, I've got PMS."

Women commonly use PMS as a defense in murder trials now. I've seen lots of cases where some ditzy broad car bombed her old man's pickup and blamed the whole thing on PMS — and the jury let her go!

Ever diligent in my research, I located Dr. Shapiro at his villa on the French Riviera where he retired on the proceeds from the sale of his book and interviewed him. He readily admitted he made the whole thing up, that it was just a scheme to sell books and enrich himself at the expense of women's gullibility.

"Oh, sure," he laughed, "I knew it was a great idea as soon as I thought of it. It was perfect! Women have always complained about their periods so all I had to do was give their complaints a name. Premenstrual syndrome popped up and I immediately ordered my broker to find me a villa on the Riviera."

"So you admit to deceiving American women?" I said.

"What deception? All I did was tell them their periods were a legitimate complaint and told them what to call it. And they loved it!"

"Well, maybe they did," I said, "but it was a fraud, you said so yourself. You made it up just so you could make money."

"Well, since when is that a crime? Look how many people it put to work. Every woman in the country bought my book and made an appointment with her doctor to get treatment and doctors logged thousands of hours of office visits as a result. Drug companies jumped on the bandwagon and brought out whole new lines of PMS medicines and their stock rose precipitously. And I got rich. What's wrong with that?"

Well, he had me there. What *is* wrong with that — aside from any moral or ethical considerations, I mean. Not a thing that I could see. The good doctor just found a need and filled it. Hell, that's the American way, isn't it?

And it is a strictly American phenomenon, you know. There hasn't been a single case of PMS reported in Europe to date, and nobody has even heard of it in all of China or India. Those places have hundreds of millions of women blithely going about their lives totally unaware of the dread ailment which has paralyzed the women of this country. Of course, I suppose they'll eventually find out about it and then they'll bedevil the hell out of their men, too.

Ah, well, that's progress for you.

Hey, I'm not being unsympathetic here, you know. Sure, it must be a pain in the ass — or in that general area, anyway — to put up with that stuff every thirty days, but women have been doing it for thousands of years without national campaigns to raise millions for research on the subject or haranguing us to death on talk shows with their chronic bitching.

Christ, you never see men on talk shows bitching about jock itch or athlete's foot, do you? We don't go around inventing new ailments so we can solicit sympathy and weasel out of our responsibilities like a lot of hypochondriacs. No, sir, we men stand tall and tough it out; we suffer silently, alone, and do our duty like real men.

I say a pox on PMS. Let's reveal this so-called disease for the sham it really is, a fraud perpetrated on an unsuspecting male population by hordes of American women trying to cop a plea in the game of life. Enough is enough. Let's boycott Donahue if he does another show on this crap. Send Oprah a message. Warn Geraldo. We're sick and tired of hearing 'em whine and moan about imagined illnesses when there are lots of real ones to complain about.

Maybe we should extradite the infamous Dr. Shapiro and haul his ass back here for trial. We could sentence him to run clinics where thousands of whining, bitching women would gather to compare symptoms and nark about what a cruel blow fate has dealt 'em.

Anyway, don't listen to her when she brings up this PMS baloney. Tell her you know all about it, refer to this book (but don't let her actually see it, of course) and cite the true facts of the matter. Let her know you aren't about to tolerate her malingering for three weeks out of every four, by God, and that's an end of it.

PMS, indeed. What do they take us for? A bunch of fools?

SURVIVAL RULES:

1. PMS is a non-disease.
2. It's strictly an American affliction; it's unknown in other countries.
3. It's used chiefly as a cop-out.
4. Flat out refuse to buy it when your wife first brings it up.
5. Get up petitions to extradite that jackass Shapiro.

Twenty-Seven

YOUR WIFE'S WEIGHT

A special chapter on your wife's weight? You're damn right, pal. I say it's a serious problem, one that isn't addressed at all from our point of view. Let's call a spade a spade here and face up to what's fast becoming a nationwide fraud so vast nothing less than a federal bunco squad can deal with it.

Look, take a gander at your wife. Go on, look at her. Now tell me, would you marry that woman if you were dating her today? Of course you wouldn't, and neither would anyone else. If you left her right now the poor creature would be destined to a life of enforced celibacy as no guy out there would give her the time of day.

She's overweight, out of shape, and something less than attractive overall. She started eating for two when she first got pregnant and she's been eating for two ever since — herself and a circus fat lady, that is. And you're stuck with her.

Do you know what this is? Fraud, that's what. When you were dating your wife she had a figure, didn't she? I mean, she actually had a waist and you could see daylight between her thighs and she bought her clothes in regular shops instead of from tent and awning manufacturers. And she led you to believe things would always be like this, that she'd continue to be attractive and desirable and sleek.

Well, she conned your ass again, didn't she? Your suspicions were aroused when she had a fourth piece of wedding cake and confirmed six months later when her doctor wanted to treat her for a case of suspected elephantiasis. The woman ate ravenously and grew exponentially and today you're saddled with two or three hundred pounds of humanity you never bargained for when you proposed.

Remember, this is the same woman you vowed (under coercion, of course) to remain faithful to for all eternity. Well, she double-crossed your ass, didn't she? This isn't the woman you married! Somebody's run in a ringer on you. You married a mere slip of a thing with long, slim legs and sexy cleavage and only one chin. You had 'scoped her out and thought, "Hey, no problem. She's a knock-out. This little filly could charm a school of religious acolytes into renouncing celibacy on the spot."

Now you look at her and find she's turned into a female sumo wrestler and all of a sudden your ardor's dampened. You have trouble getting it up on occasion, and when you do you feel something's missing, that it just isn't the same anymore. And then you see the girl next door out weeding the flower bed in short-shorts and a halter top that consists of two square inches of cloth and a lot of string. Your libido begins imagining the unimag- inable and before you know it you find yourself entangled in an adulterous affair *and whose fault is it?*

Surely not yours. You acted in good faith, you upheld your end of the bargain, but your wife didn't. She said, "Who cares now? I got my man. What's the difference if I put on a few pounds? Who am I trying to impress? Cut me another wedge of that cake, Thelma."

I ask you, is this fair? Isn't this fraud of some kind? Haven't you been deceived, tricked, conned, bamboozled, swindled and hoodwinked? Certainly you have, we all have, and I say we shouldn't take it anymore, by God! I say we should launch a national campaign to force fat wives to get in some kind of damn shape and do it now.

Okay, I can hear all the heavyweights out there bitching and carping about how I'm an insensitive slob with a heart of stone who doesn't know the awful trauma these poor things suffer by being overweight. They've all got metabolism problems or it's genetic and can't be helped or they're emotionally distraught and need succor or it's compulsive and beyond their control.

Bullcrap. The old bats eat too damn much, that's the problem. Tell 'em to stop eating and watch the pounds melt away. No fancy diets are needed, no chocolate vitamin drinks at six bucks a quart, no powders or syrups or anti-cholesterol depressants or fat gram emulsifiers or low fat simulators or any similar "diet aid" is required. All you have to do is stop shoving four thousand calories a day down your gullets, for Christ's sake.

I say a man's entitled to the wife he married and not some obese imposter who shows up later claiming to be the original model. I mean, a lot of us husbands may be a little slow, but we sure as hell can recognize our own wives when we see 'em. Let's get the real ones back. Maybe we'll be more inclined to keep our lunchhooks off all the Miss Sloe-eyeds out there then.

What's that? Do I hear some woman complaining that her husband's something less — or more — than the man she married? You say your husband has put on twenty or thirty pounds and what's sauce for the goose is sauce for the gander and all that?

Okay, maybe that's so, but it isn't the same thing, is it? I mean, everybody knows it's more important for women to maintain their figures than it is for men. Why, there's even something to be said for a nice, well-developed corporation on a successful man; it gives him a certain air, a feeling of stability and presence and worth.

In fact, it could be said that men need a little extra heft, as it were. Remember scheming Cassius being referred to as a man who "hath a lean and hungry look"? While that's the exact look that wears well on women, it isn't entirely suitable for men. Hell, no less a figure than Shakespeare himself said so.

Besides, men look better with a few extra pounds than women do. You put a heavy-set guy in a suit or sport coat and he looks just fine, but you can't say the same for women in dresses or — heaven forbid! — pants. We've all seen these female behemoths rolling down the street looking like two hundred pounds of sausage stuffed into a sack designed to hold half that amount, and we'll never forget it, either.

Another point, women don't look at men the way we do women. (They don't because, as we've already seen, most women don't give a rap about sex and men do.) I mean, guys watch women, and they do it all the time, too. We watch 'em getting in and out of cars, walking along the street, riding bikes, sitting, jogging in those incredibly short shorts and thin tops sans bras.

We watch 'em in magazines and ads and movies and on TV and billboards and everywhere we can find 'em. We want to see women with nice figures and great boobs and slim waists and long, slim nylon-clad legs and sexy cleavage and racy under-wear and high heels and...

Well, you see what I mean. You'd think since women know they're under constant scrutiny they'd want to look their best, but still they insist on eating themselves into objects of disdain to the girl-watchers of the world.

And another point. Women need good looks to attract and hold men and everybody knows that's true. It has to do with primal urges and atavistic leanings and brain chemistry and isn't just a condition created by advertisers who use this knowledge to sell stuff. Cave men were all voyeurs who spent half their time hiding in bushes ogling cave girls at their daily river baths. And ancient Roman school boys tried to look under the girls' togas just as modern boys do dresses today.

Show a guy a naked girl or a stretch of flashing thigh or a glimpse of cleavage or a bunch of tangled nudes in a perfume ad and you'll have the poor sap's attention in its entirety. He can't help it. Sanctified preachers and monks on sabbatical and church choir members and Sunday school superintendents and Boy Scout troop leaders are all vulnerable and will gape in open-mouthed wonder at a set of bare boobs.

That being the case, isn't it to women's advantage to keep themselves looking just as great as they possibly can? Wouldn't they get a better shake from men (including their husbands) if they took the trouble to preserve the body they married the guy in?

Well, you guys out there can do something about this, too. The secret is still to start in the beginning and nip those extra pounds in the damn bud. Say your wife is 120 on your wedding day. Okay. Note her weight, write it down somewhere and date the entry so you can refer to it years later. Then check her weight regularly. You can do this unobtrusively by pretending to get a new bar of soap or something just as she mounts the scale.

Or, confront her. Put her ass on the scale by main force if you have to and let her know you give a damn how much she weighs and demand to know it to the pound. If she gains a few pounds, tell her so. Nag her. If you don't know how to nag, listen to her and you'll pick it up soon enough. Don't let her weight soar. It's up to you, you can control your own destiny if you really want to.

Leave her to her own devices, though, and she'll blimp out on your ass every time. She really will. A word to the wise, as they say.

SURVIVAL RULES:

1. **Most wives are overweight.**
2. **We're victims of fraud; we married slim girls and ended up with two hundred pound strangers.**
3. **Insist on the return of the original model.**
4. **The solution is simplicity itself: STOP EATING.**
5. **Monitor her weight from day one. Tolerate no increase.**
6. **A "corporation" on a man is a mark of distinction.**

Twenty-Eight

THE BEST VACATIONS

If your wife is like most others, she'll want to take joint vacations and it's okay to go along with this to a degree. If you're still talking to each other after you've been married a year and that first vacation comes around, go ahead and take her to Toledo to see her cousins or whatever, but allow for a solo three day fishing break for yourself. It's still another case of setting patterns, that's all.

Eventually, things will change until you long for a respite from marital cares and you can angle for separate vacations. Drop some subtle hints. Mention articles you come across which extol separate vacations, leave pamphlets on famous beach resorts lying around (or whatever particular kind of vacation she fancies) while you regularly bring up the delights to be found in trout fishing in cold mountain streams.

In other words, establish dual interests. As each new vacation rolls around you suggest how much you'd like to hit that old mountain stream in the high Rockies this year. Don't worry, she won't go. Most wives hate cold mountain streams because they're never close to shopping malls or good hairdressers. She'll flatly refuse and you pout a bit and mope around the garage with your fly rod and really work the guilt angle to prey on her conscience.

Yeah, I know, most wives haven't got a conscience, but you're slyly encouraging her that she'd have a really great time doing girl things with her friend Elsie in Fort Lauderdale or wherever. When she finally consents to separate vacations, it won't be to humor you but rather to do herself a service. That's how wives are, that's all.

Meanwhile, you keep taking those weekend fishing trips. Get her used to the idea of your going off with a couple of buddies on a regular basis and it'll be a lot easier for her to adjust to a week in the high Rockies later. Remember, though, to actually bring some fish home as evidence that you're really fishing and not playing fast and loose with a lot of bimbos somewhere. Of course, it isn't necessary that you actually catch the fish you bring home. A quick stop at the local fish market will provide all the evidence you need.

Be careful, though. A husband must never relax his guard lest he make a fatal mistake and blow the whole thing. A friend of mine came back from a weekend "fishing trip" in Atlantic City once and stopped by the fish market for evidence of his piscatory prowess and he mistakenly picked up five or six nice halibut. The only thing is he was supposed to be fishing in Lake Michigan and halibut are ocean fish rarely found in fresh water lakes. Needless to say, that ended the poor sap's fishing trips.

You also want to remember not to bring things home that could be used as evidence against your ass in a court of law. For instance, don't have any left over casino chips in your pockets, or stubs from Vegas shows, or phone numbers on matchbook covers, or similar souvenirs which might indicate you were nowhere near the banks of any trout stream.

If you play your cards right, by your fifth anniversary you should be taking annual Caribbean cruises on swinging-singles-only cruise ships or laughing it up in Las Vegas casinos and consorting with show girls. It's all in the wrist, you know.

Just remember to arrive back home clad in your hip boots and plaid shirt with your fly rod and tackle in hand. We've all heard of the joker who went "hunting" and left his gun at home and never even missed it.

Such a thing is even harder to explain than ocean fish in Lake Michigan. Prepare a few tales with which to regale your wife to complete the deception. Tell her long, boring stories about the quest for Ol' Spot, the legendary giant trout of the upper branch of Rocky Point Creek and how you finally hooked the bastard and fought up and down the banks of the creek for six full hours only to lose him when he snagged your line around an old stump and broke it off, etc.

She'll be bored to death, of course, and won't even listen to the whole story, but that's okay since all you want to do is lend authenticity to your lie anyway.

It's a good idea to contact various distant resorts, fishing camps, guide outfits, and so on so you can have a supply of brochures on hand in a large file folder. Pore over them in the evening when she's looking on to further establish your bogus interest in fishing. Hold a brochure in your hand and gaze wistfully through the window as though you're envisioning a rousing fight with Ol' Spot in some pristine mountain setting. Sigh audibly.

I've known old-timers who've pulled these tricks for a quarter century and longer and the old lady never got wise. They've caroused in half the high sin zones in America, taken cruises everywhere, played golf on the best courses from coast to coast, gambled and gamboled and smoked cigars and drank Scotch and never wet a line the whole time, and all because they took the trouble to figure out an angle and work out the details ahead of time.

And you can do the same. Start collecting travel brochures today, buy a fly rod and a bunch of string and feathers and tie a few flies, wear a fishing vest and putz around in the garage to simulate an interest in fishing. Send her off alone every chance you get so she'll be used to going without you. Talk it up with her girlfriends.

Inveigle, connive, and deceive and you too can add a little spice to your life and make the whole thing worthwhile.

SURVIVAL RULES:

1. **Suggest a week-long fishing trip in the high Rockies for your first vacation but let her have her way.**
2. **Set pattern early of solo weekend fishing trips. Always bring back fish.**
3. **Gradually establish dual interests.**
4. **Encourage her to take solo trips with friends, relatives.**
5. **Tie flies, order brochures, sigh wistfully as proof of your interest in fishing.**
6. **Be careful. No poker chips, airline tickets to Vegas, etc. in your pockets.**
7. **Set deadline. Solo Caribbean cruises within five years.**

Twenty-Nine

TRIAL SEPARATIONS

If your marriage is like most others — and it is — you'll both be thoroughly pissed with each other by the end of, say, the third year at the latest and this is the perfect time to suggest a trial separation. Of course, you'll imply that you're anxious to preserve your marriage and are doing this only as a last resort, and this may well be true, but what you really want is a little time on your own so you can have some fun again for a change.

In fact, before this comes up you should have been through counseling with good ol' Tony so you can enlist his aid in pulling this off. Just tell him a friend of yours was in a trial separation mode and you wondered if it might be an option for the two of you. Tony will get the hint because he's anxious to please you and keep you coming back at seventy-five bucks an hour and he'll approve the idea.

Your wife may object but you stick to your guns. Go right out and rent a suitable bachelor pad and move in before she has time to martial her forces. Announce to all your single buddies that you're back in business. Get out your old address book (you *did* save it, didn't you?) and start punching in numbers and make the most of your hiatus from the marital wars.

You'll be astonished at the reaction of the single women out there. They're like vultures circling over every marriage with a steely eye on the lookout for any signs of discord which may give 'em an opening to swoop in and snatch up some other woman's husband. As I said earlier, they have no moral code or sense of honor when it comes to stealing each others' men. There's no feminine version of the Geneva Convention for their sex, no idea of fair play or rules; it's every broad for herself and the loser is an old maid.

So they'll be delighted to hear you're splitsville with your wife. Oh, they'll say how sorry they are to hear about it and all that crap, but it's a damn lie. Her misfortune is their opportunity. The sneaky broads will bombard your ass with plates of cookies and "extra" tickets to hockey games and home-cooked meals prepared by their conniving mothers who don't have any morals, either. You'll experience deception and double-dealing that would make Rasputin look like a damn choir boy, for God's sake.

But most of all you'll be offered nooky. Every modern woman knows the real way to a man's heart is through nooky and lots of it. The wanton creatures will make no bones about it, either. As soon as they hear you're up for grabs again, they'll call *you*. You'll have to step lively to keep 'em from getting in each other's way and may even have to employ an answering service to sort out the incoming calls.

Well, it's just what you wanted, isn't it? You're on the loose, your time's your own, and you don't have to answer to anyone. Isn't that incredible? The condemned man suddenly pardoned, reprieved, given a new lease on life and sent out into the world for a second chance at living. What more could a man ask?

A word of caution, though. Remember, you're dealing with some of the most unscrupulous people on the planet, women so depraved and amoral that they'll stop at nothing to con you into a permanent liaison with them so they can assume the wifely role and abuse your ass for their own merriment. You must be always on the alert if you aren't going to end up divorced and remarried almost before you've had a chance to enjoy your new-found freedom.

Since this is only meant to be a trial separation and you intend to go home once you've enjoyed the fruits of a little freedom, you have to keep things percolating at home. Keep in touch with your wife. Meet on neutral ground at Tony's and keep the lines of communication open at least enough that she doesn't file for divorce on you. Make progress reports but don't supply all the details.

You've got to make her think this is very traumatic for you, that you're living a lonely and sobering life in a cramped apartment without cable TV or any of the amenities. Imply that your social life is centered around checker games at the "Y" and lonely nights with TV and bouts of soul-searching introspection. It'll cheer her up to think you miss her and help smooth things out when you finally come home.

Remember that your wife won't be having all the fun you are since she's got more at stake in all this than you have. For one thing, her mother'll be on her ass because she's afraid her daughter'll get a divorce and move back home and she can't stand her any more than you can.

And your wife won't be out every night with handsome jocks or carousing in all the spots with the beautiful people since all that presupposes an escort and she won't have one. Let's face it, there aren't all that many handsome, eligible guys out there for separated wives to hustle. If one did show up you can bet dozens of anxiety-ridden dames would be hot on his trail and your wife'd be just another bimbo trying to snare a man.

I know that's not a pretty picture for women but it's an accurate one. Guys don't flock around the way predatory women do since we aren't looking to snare anybody and therefore don't acquire that aura of desperation that afflicts women in their unrelenting pursuit of husbands.

Whatever you do, don't let her find out about all the nooky that's coming your way. Once she finds out you're getting laid seven nights a week with occasional matinee performances thrown in for good measure, she'll call the whole thing off and demand you get your ass home *now!* What's more, she'll never fall for this dodge again; you won't be able to work a separate vacation or even a weekend fishing trip. In fact, you'll be lucky if she doesn't put your ass on permanent house arrest.

To help in this, don't tell her where you live. Insist it's better that way. Tell her the whole point of a trial separation is to be separated and that means no contact whatsoever for the first, uh, say three months. Get affable Tony to back you up on this and you're home free.

With any luck at all, in three months you'll be exhausted to the point of near collapse from all the orgies, late nights, and riotous living, and in need of a rest. Okay, so get rid of eight or ten of the least pretty girls and slack off on things. Do it gradually, of course, and preferably under a doctor's direction. Remember, a sudden decrease in nooky could shock the nervous system and severely damage the psyche.

Then you can start patching things up on the home front. Start seeing your wife again. Drop by for a nice home-cooked meal once in a while and bring her flowers and all that crap. Hint that you've been thinking and maybe you should get back together again pretty soon (be vague here unless you're ready to move back in that night). Go back to see Tony and let him suggest a reconciliation. In order to offer maximum protection to your psyche, it should be some time sufficiently far off to allow you to reduce your sex life gradually until you reach your pre-trial separation rate of twice a month.

Then you move back home and everything's hunky-dory again.

* * *

One final note here lest people think I'm advocating some unconscionable exploitation of women merely to gratify our own libidos. Nothing could be further from the truth. Like most American men, I hold women in the highest esteem in spite of the fact that many of them are predators who spend all their time trying to take over our lives and rob us of our very selves. I wish them no harm and even hope for their success — just so it's not at my expense, of course.

But let's recognize it for what it is: It's us against them in a battle of wits and chemistry and nature, each of us using the weapons at his or her disposal and fighting under nobody's rules and without quarter given or taken. So nature has decreed it.

And you need a marital sabbatical, a reprieve from the rigors of connubial bliss, a chance to catch your breath, as it were. Hell, even soldiers in combat are rotated out on R&R leaves to keep 'em from running amuck and the stress of modern marriage is at least as great as in any mere war.

Periodic breaks in the routine will enable you to maintain a fresh view of things and keep a solid grip on your sanity — and make the whole thing worthwhile.

And I might add in passing that these separations will also benefit your wife since she's doubtless under certain pressures living with a guy like you and she'll enjoy the change, too. In fact, it's a good idea to convince her the whole thing's being done for her sake as she'll take to the idea quicker if she thinks that.

Wasn't it ever thus?

So be it.

SURVIVAL RULES:

1. Aim for your first trial separation after about three years.

2. Enlist your marriage counselor (Tony) to help pull it off.

3. Move out. Get a bachelor pad.

4. Don't tell her where it is.

5. Beware of single women as they're unscrupulous and will be after your ass.

6. Don't let her know you're enjoying yourself.

7. Remember to taper off before going back home. Do so under a doctor's supervision.

8. Begin laying plans immediately for the next trial separation three or four years down the road.

Thirty

BEAUTY SHOPS

A lot of guys get pissed when their wives fuss around too much with cosmetics and hairdressers and whatnot, and with good reason, too. This kind of stuff can break a guy if carried to the extreme. Imagine shipping your wife off to one of those resorts where they lay out two or three grand a week for mud baths, steam cleaning, and massages from slippery looking Italians in tight-fitting pants.

That's okay if you're rich and don't give a damn, but it's not for us working stiffs. Oh, sure, it'd be nice to pack the missus away for a whole week so we could get in a little extra pool or golf or even a quick sweep through the flesh pots downtown, but three grand is a lot of money to pay for a few days off. Besides, think how many cigars you could buy with that much money.

Okay, so resorts are out, but let's not panic over your wife's general maintenance program. While it costs a small fortune, it's worth it if it does any good. See, the problem with most wives is they don't give a damn once they've snagged some poor klutz and have his ass neatly sewn up in legal and spiritual red tape and they let themselves go straight to hell physically. Not only do they gain weight at a rate that rivals pubescent rhinos, but they deteriorate in every other way.

With that in mind, it's not an altogether bad thing if they spend a little on upkeep in the form of nail polish, hairdos, false eyelashes, and so on. At least they're making an effort to be presentable and that's worth something.

She'll probably have her hair done weekly and it'll set you back twenty or thirty bucks each time. Include manicures and pedicures and it adds up to over a grand a year just to get haircuts, and if that seems a little steep remember that it also includes marital advice, psychological counseling, and an update on local goings-on. Actually, it's cheap at the price.

Women are totally different from guys about these things. A guy goes to the barbershop, thumbs through a year-old copy of Field and Stream, gets a fifteen minute haircut, and blows the place. Nine times out of ten the only words he'll utter will be, "Cut it the same, Jake."

Women couldn't possibly do that. With them a trip to the hairdresser is an event. They have standing appointments so they always see the same women each time they go and know 'em intimately. Gossip is the order of the day. They chatter on about who's getting a divorce, having an affair, dying, moving, operations, husbands, work, soaps and movies, and each other.

They never discuss politics, the world scene, advances in science or technology, the historicity of religion, the latest Nobel laureates, or anything else of substance. In fact, matters of substance are banned in beauty shops by some sort of international feminine agreement so any woman can enter any beauty shop in the world and rest assured that no one will test her mental acuity by bringing up any subject other than gossip.

The customers also serve as support groups for each other and offer advice and counseling without cost or obligation. If your wife's thinking of throwing your ass out on the street, her cronies at the hairdresser's will know of it long before you do. They'll analyze your faults in great detail, discuss alternate plans of action, and recommend good divorce lawyers.

The widows and single ones will also note that her husband (you), the very one they're all urging her to dump, will soon be available and begin laying plans to swoop in and claim your ass for their very own. As I said before, they have no scruples.

And women love these places. My wife would sooner miss the social event of the year than blow a hair appointment. She'll drive through a raging blizzard —and has!— to keep her Thursday afternoon appointment at Pierre's Salon de Beauté. I've seen her crawl out of her sick bed and haul herself across town rather than miss her weekly meeting with "the girls".

Actually, these beauty shops become an adjunct of the home, a center for social activities, a kind of club where old bats can go to let off steam and commiserate with each other over the unfairness of life and your shortcomings. They're a kind of mental health spa and help 'em keep a grip on themselves, and when considered in that light they're a bargain for fifteen hundred or so a year.

Of course, beauty shops are only a part of the average wife's maintenance expenses. They're forever buying lipstick, rouge, eyeliner, mascara, dry skin cream, various powders and ointments and tonics, and sundry items designed to make 'em glamorous. No one's ever uncovered the true cost of all this junk but it's got to be a helluva lot of money over a year's time. If plowed into sound securities, you'd be able to retire a good ten years earlier.

But I say let 'em have it and consider yourself lucky. At the very least it means she's trying to maintain some part of her looks and that's a plus for you. After all, if the old crone never went to a beauty shop and made a single tube of lipstick last a year, she'd likely be a pretty grim-looking specimen and not one you'd find very appealing in things sexual.

If she doesn't care enough about her appearance to do some work on it, you'll end up with an ugly old broad in a shabby housedress, stringy hair tied in a knot, run-down slippers, and an overall demeanor that'll drive you to voluntary celibacy or worse. Isn't that a fate worse than death?

So I say pack the missus off to the beauty shop. Sign her up for a lifetime membership, enroll her ass in mail-order beauty programs, hire people to make her over every six months or so, encourage her to preserve whatever beauty she has left. Not only will she be grateful for such support, but you'll have a wife you can take out in public where people see her and not have to pretend she isn't with you.

How many guys can say that?

SURVIVAL RULES:

1. **Women love beauty parlors.**
2. **Encourage your wife to go for**
   a. **makeup**
   b. **hairdo**
   c. **and manicures, support, gossip, psychological counseling, an active social life, and advice to the lovelorn.**
3. **Remember, it's cheap at the price.**
4. **Never ask what she talks about there. (It's probably you.)**

Thirty-One

YOUR WIFE AND
THE OCCULT

I don't know why it is, but most women seem to be suckers for weird things like ghosts, tarot cards, tea leaf readings, fortunetellers, psychics and similar scams. Astrology is big with 'em, too. They seem to have some basic need to believe in magic.

Maybe it comes from that fairy prince crap they all get when they're little girls. They grow up believing there are knights in shining armor who sweep in and rescue pretty girls and carry 'em away to castles and lives of luxury and ease for no other reason than that they're pretty. Jesus, you'd think they'd wise up when they grow up and marry guys with pot bellies and halitosis who carry 'em off to tract houses in some dreary suburb somewhere.

But they never learn. Get a gaggle of women together for a day on the town and they immediately look for some fraudulent tea leafer or two-bit psychic they can pay twenty-five bucks apiece for a look at their "fortunes". The old grafter feeds 'em a lot of generalized nonsense about tall, dark strangers and who they were in previous lives (always a princess, of course), and they come away all smiles and perfectly satisfied with the results.

Amazing.

The harm comes when your wife gets hooked on some swami or star-gazer and starts paying over larger sums of cash to him and, even worse, begins ordering her life — and yours — around some kind of wacky celestial navigation. Look at Nancy Reagan. She had poor old Ron waiting for propitious "signs" to schedule his next summit conference and when people found it out the president was made to look ridiculous.

Your wife may even try to involve you in this malarkey but don't you let her. If she asks you to attend her next seance, go along only for the ride but try not to laugh and spoil the fun for everyone else. For some of 'em it's pretty heady stuff and it unnerves 'em when somebody bursts out laughing smack in the middle of Grandma's soliloquy from the other side.

A clever man might use his wife's infatuation with the occult to his own advantage, and I knew one who tried. This guy knew his wife and her girlfriends were going to see a certain psychic and he stopped by to see the guy first. He gave him an extra fifty to tell her her husband needed more exercise to head off some sort of heart trouble. The psychic also said he saw her husband on a golf course three times a week and his heart was back to normal.

It didn't work, though. You see, the guy's wife hated golf and bitched every time he played. What he didn't know was that women never hear anything at these readings they don't want to hear so the golf yarn never registered. The last I heard he was down to nine holes a month and his wife was running ads to sell his clubs.

"YOU WOULDN'T BELIEVE WHAT
HAPPENED TO ME AT WORK TODAY!"

Don't deride her for her loony beliefs because it'll just piss her off and make her even more intractable. Still, you should be firm in refusing to give any credence to the stuff or she'll be encouraged and get even more involved. An occasional outing with the girls is okay, but watch for signs of addiction. If she's playing solitaire with tarot cards or casting her horoscope before going to the market, it may be time to call a screeching halt to the proceedings.

By the way, in case your wife brings it up, there's no correlation between the bogus hocus-pocus world of the occult and such universally recognized realities as luck or body english applied to a bowling ball in flight or hunches and similar natural phenomena. Everyone knows these things work. For instance, I knew a guy who caught the number seven bus and got off at Seventh Street. Well, he looked at his transfer and it had four sevens on it and he realized it was the seventh day of the seventh month!

Now, it happens that his horse finished seventh in the seventh race, but that doesn't mean the hunch wasn't any good. Only a complete fool would pass up all those sevens. It's obvious lady luck was trying to tell him something and he probably just mixed up the signals. In fact, it happened that there was a fight that night at the Armory and the main event ended with a knockout in the seventh round!

See what I mean?

SURVIVAL RULES:

1. Most women love the occult because...
2. ...most women are gullible.
3. Don't accompany her. You'll only laugh and cause trouble.
4. Bribe the psychic (guru, seer, etc.) to your advantage.
5. Don't deride her "hobby". It'll just piss her off.
6. Unlike the occult, hunches, body english, and luck are not mere superstition and buncombe but proven scientific laws.

Thirty-Two

GAMBLING WIVES

Everybody knows gambling can be a serious problem for a lot of people, and that it's usually men who are the victims. Women can get to the track or call a bookie just as easily as any man, but they don't because the average woman isn't much interested in horses or crap games. Most of 'em would rather shop.

Women do like casinos where they can pump their life savings into slot machines or play black-jack at the two dollar table for hours on end, but that's usually not a problem for the average guy since there aren't any casinos nearby for his wife to get at and flying to Atlantic City or Vegas isn't all that convenient. Still, there are other ways for your wife to catch the gambling fever and render you an impecunious bankrupt almost overnight.

Lots of women nowadays launch gambling careers by playing state lotteries and it's almost impossible to stop 'em since temptation and opportunity are everywhere. Supermarket check-out clerks offer lotto tickets instead of change and every 7-Eleven, drugstore, and shopping mall has a lottery franchise. It's small wonder our poor, gullible wives are turned into candidates for Gamblers Anonymous right before our very eyes.

Still, there isn't a lot of fun in lotteries since it's a solitary activity without the trappings and social attractions of, say, the track or a glitzy casino or a card parlor with guys wearing green eyeshades and pinkie rings. I mean, where's the glamour in scratching lotto tickets on a bench in the mall?

So your wife may get started on lotteries and even put a pretty fair dent in your budget over the years, but the real danger lies in getting addicted to some of the more insidious games of chance that are out there. The most dangerous period usually comes after she's been married for enough years to discover your true self and, thoroughly disillusioned, looks elsewhere for meaning in her life.

And that's where bingo comes in. Your wife doesn't have to go any further than the nearest church or VFW hall to get caught up in this deadly pastime. Believe me, there are few things worse than a bingo-playing wife. It's a pernicious disease, one which is all-consuming and even more addictive than heroin.

These bingo games occur most often in the local churches and they're big business. I've known some good-sized cathedrals that were given over almost entirely to gambling and drew enormous crowds every week as regularly as clockwork. They were outfitted with crap tables, jai-alai frontons, bingo halls, and OTB parlors while dozens of croupiers, dealers, pit bosses and drink girls worked the crowds.

Outside, huge searchlights probed the night sky and lighted the way to at least five or six of the seven deadly sins. Valets parked the cars, off-duty cops directed traffic, people queued up on the sidewalk waiting to get in, and church officials piously looked on and smiled the smile of businessmen pleased with the day's take.

Just drop around to the church hall some evening and watch the girls in action and you'll see what I mean. By the way, they're nearly all women, too. Guys don't like bingo; I don't know why that is but it's true. All bingo halls are filled to the gunnels with women of a certain age, which is to say over forty. Most of 'em are somewhat the worse for wear and have completely exhausted their supplies of pheromones. Come to think of it, maybe that's why guys don't like bingo much. After all, who wants to hang around with a bunch of ugly broads sans pheromones?

Bingo halls all have a certain atmosphere about 'em. For one thing, the air's filled with smoke because two-thirds of the players smoke up a storm. Ashtrays are everywhere and filled to overflowing. There's a pervasive background noise made up of muffled curses, flicking lighters, hacking coughs, and spinning balls in wire cages. The voice of the guy in charge rings out hollowly and monotonously and the whole place takes on a kind of surreal aura.

But the thing to watch is the action at the tables. There are long tables stretching across the room and all the way to the back wall. Hundreds of women sit hunched over their cards, ashtray near at hand and a stack of markers piled to one side. The caller occupies a place at the front of the room and calls numbers into a mike.

And look at 'em go! Each woman has several cards, anywhere from four or five to a dozen or more and they scan 'em faster than the best computer could. Here you have old ladies who are in the later stages of Alzheimer's disease and they can memorize hundreds of numbers and cover called ones with lightning speed.

"B-9!" the caller sings out, and hundreds of eye-balls fly over the cards and nimble fingers dart out and drop markers everywhere and when the next number is called two seconds later everybody's waiting impatiently for it. None of 'em ever miss a beat, no one looks up, no one goes to the john. You couldn't distract 'em with a three-alarm blaze in the center of the room.

Before long someone shouts "Bingo!" and every-body else says, "Oh, hell!" or something and the room suddenly buzzes with talk as people clear away losing cards and get ready for the next round.

Incidentally, there's always some clown who declares he has a bingo and everybody dumps his cards and it turns out the jerk's drunk or some-thing and he doesn't have a bingo after all. This never happens with women; they're too tenacious, too dedicated to make a mistake. When a woman shouts bingo the game's over, period.

As I said, bingo's addictive. I've heard of six or seven old bats piling into a van and hitting the bin-go circuit on a swing through half a dozen nearby states and blowing thousands of dollars in the process. Husbands are abandoned, homes left unattended, life savings drained away in a mad pursuit of bingo nirvana. It's an oft-told story, heart-wrenching and sad, and it could be yours.

One advantage of her gambling addiction is that you know your wife's completely faithful. Gamblers just don't give a damn about sex. They're so wrapped up in bingo cards, blackjack, black or red, full-houses, boxcars and all the rest that lurid sexual thoughts never cross their minds. You can test this at any track between races. Robert Redford could stroll past the stands on ladies' day and not one of 'em would look up from her program.

It's even true with guys. The sexiest of women dressed in next to nothing will hardly cause a stir with a lot of guys who are trying to work out a trifecta. Oh, I don't mean they're zombies or asexual or anything — no guy is ever completely asexual — but all the doll will get is a long, appreciative glance and then it's back to the Racing Form. Isn't that kind of power over man scary as hell, though?

So keep the little woman away from the lure of the gaming tables. Oh, it's okay once in a while to take her along on one of your Vegas gambols and let her have a go at the slots for a day or two. She'll lose a few hundred bucks and discolor her fingers all the way up to her elbows and get the whole business out of her system for another year or two. That way she'll think you're a prince for even taking her along and maybe you can limit the huge losses you'd suffer if she was hanging out at the local track.

By the way, it may have occurred to you that all this could be avoided if you were careful to follow the warning in the chapter on money and saw to it that you were in charge of the ready cash. If you dole out her allowance each week there's no way she could blow your assets in lotteries or bingo games since she wouldn't have any to blow. She'd have to come back to you for more cash and you'd demand to know what the hell she did with her allowance and that'd be that.

Of course, she could begin selling off the silverware and filching money from your wallet while you're in the shower, but that would hardly sustain a major gambling habit. After all, how much silverware does the average family have?

So, anyway, keep an eye on your wife and don't let her play the lottery or bingo. Of course, this means she can't go to church, either, since that's where most of the bingo halls are located. If her moral fibre suffers from a lack of spiritual guidance and she goes to hell, well, that's not your fault, is it?

In fact, it seems to me the churches bear some responsibility if their parishioners turn into gambling addicts and bring themselves and their families to economic ruin and spiritual damnation. It might be a good idea if they set a better example and held pancake breakfasts and prayer outings as a means of raising revenue and lightened up on commercializing sin and debauchery.

But what the hell do I know?

SURVIVAL RULES:

1. **Beware of the gambler's curse; it's a disease.**
2. **Don't live too close to Vegas or Atlantic City.**
3. **Keep your wife away from churches.**
4. **If she's a gambling freak, she's not having an affair.**
5. **Count the silverware regularly.**

Thirty-Three

WIVES ON DRUGS

Is your wife likely to be a sneak coke sniffer? Or a dope smoker on the sly? Will she shoot heroin? Probably not, but that doesn't mean she isn't on dope.

I'm talking about prescription drugs, the ones her doctor provides. You know, tranquilizers, uppers and downers, reds and yellows and greenies, anti-depressants and stimulators and levellers-out and all the rest. She may well be hooked on these things and you never suspect a thing. Most wives have medicine chests full of pills and whatnot and most husbands never pay any attention to what they are. We just figure they must be for some sort of female complaint and go on with our own affairs.

Yet, who knows? How to account for violent mood swings? A wife who seems fairly rational at noon becomes a raging maniac when you come home at three a.m. What happens to cause this? Surely that isn't the behavior of a normal woman — or is it?

Or what about strange emotional behavior? I read somewhere that the average woman cries six or seven times a month, for God's sake. What the hell's going on out there? Is this rational? And what are they crying about? Is it possible they're all on something?

How is it she can drop off in a dead sleep and sleep like a dead woman straight through till noon the following day? Sleeping pills? But why doesn't she ever show any signs of life, especially in the sex department? Is it because she's *not* on pep pills?

Or is TV a drug? When your wife watches soaps, can you hear the synapses snapping in her head from across the room? Is Dallas an addictive drug that clouds women's minds and affects their judgment?

The answer to all of the above is a resounding *yes*. In spite of all Nancy Reagan could do, American women are zonked out on a variety of substances that make 'em almost impossible for the average poor slob to deal with. Along with the natural irrationality peculiar to their sex, they've added chemical and electronic factors unheard of just a few short years ago. If this trend continues much longer, all communication between the sexes will break down entirely and society will be forced to adopt some sort of sexual apartheid to keep us from killing each other.

So we get rid of drugs, eh? Not so fast here. If your wife is denied her daily dose of General Hospital, what'll that do to her disposition? Or will the loss of her nerve pills result in non-stop nagging and your own eventual mental collapse?

Obviously, we have to tread lightly here or we're liable to come up with a cure worse than the disease. In fact, maybe we should be going in exactly the opposite direction. Wouldn't it be to your advantage if your wife's mind was on General Hospital instead of finding new ways to make your life a living hell? If she's zeroed in on Donahue and Oprah and the soaps, the old bat won't have time for you and that's got to be a plus for the average guy.

You could go a step further and buy her more TV sets. Get her one of those Walkman sets so she can have her soaps wherever she goes and she'll never have a clear thought again. Finish her off with lifetime subscriptions to People Magazine and the National Enquirer and she'll lose her own personality and become something else — and whatever it is, it's bound to be an improvement over the present model.

Now this may seem a radical scheme to some people out there, mostly ones who aren't married to your wife, but it really isn't. After all, don't we regularly use various chemicals, electric shock, hypnosis, acupuncture, psychoanalysis, and other bizarre schemes to control and modify human behavior? Why, modern psychiatry would have to close up shop altogether if we took away their drug therapies, light sockets, and upscale voodoo.

Come to think of it, we may have hit on something revolutionary here. Why not a whole new science directed at rendering wives harmless? It might even be possible to make 'em companionable, turn 'em into people we'd actually enjoy having around. Okay, maybe that's asking for too much, but it'd be a major step forward in man's evolution as a species if we could just make 'em tolerable, wouldn't it?

Mothers-in-law could be hypnotized at the reception and turned into reasonably pleasant people, for instance. And they could be kept that way from then on and never allowed to do any harm. What a boon for humanity that would be! Countless marriages would be saved from this idea alone and unnumbered husbands spared ulcers and great emotional stress just by rendering mothers-in-law *hors-de-combat* forever.

Imagine a world of the future, a world where man rules supreme just as God intended him to. (You don't think that's what He had in mind? Check out the Old Testament then.) In this bright tomorrow a man who wanted, say, to play golf with his buddies for the third time in four days would just burn some incense and mumble a few incantations and the old bat'd willingly shine up his clubs and help him load 'em into the trunk.

With a mind-controlled wife the philanderer could philander to his heart's content, the fisherman fish away whole summers, golfers golf and drinkers drink and pool players play without wifely intervention. Wouldn't that be the grandest of grand worlds?

So here's the plan. Find a voodooist and enlist his support. Be sure he's married and you'll know he's sympathetic. Find out which incense work best for golf outings, fishing trips, or weekends away with your secretary and lay in a supply of the stuff along with the mandatory doll and collection of pins. Start her off gradually and add new pins as she builds a tolerance to 'em and cut yourself a little slack, for God's sake.

There *is* hope for mankind if we can just get a grip on our wives.

NB — Hey, all you doctors out there. Here's a new specialty, one that'll enrich you beyond your wildest dreams: Wife control. Come up with a scheme to keep wives under wraps and render 'em more or less harmless. Run ads in the sports section offering safe and efficient ways to neutralize wives and guys will turn that well-worn path to your door into a major freeway. You'll have to open branch offices all over town to handle the business and you could be retired to the Riviera years before your already lucrative practices will get you there.

Men everywhere will rejoice and applaud your efforts and heap honors on your ass and cap it all with a Nobel and the cover of Time. Move society back to the wisdom of the Old Testament and restore man's rightful place as ruler of planet Earth and your name will resound down through the annals of time.

Astonishing.

And don't forget my ten percent for the idea.

As an aside, it just occurred to me that a devious, conniving, and completely amoral wife could do the same to you! I mean, what's to stop her from turning you into a damn zombie and using your ass for a doorstop while she runs amuck at the mall or gets bingo fixes six nights a week? We know wives are capable of such deceit; we've already seen where they have no moral sense and would even take delight in such activity.

What to do? Easy. First, check with the voodoo people and buy an amulet, one of those charms designed to ward off evil spirits and marauding wives. Wear the thing night and day and she won't be able to hex you with her own magic.

Better yet, strike first. Get her before she reads this book and can swing into action with her own plan. Check with that voodist first thing in the morning and get a jump on the old bat. If you act fast, you can have her under complete control within a fortnight and be safe from any counterplot.

Unbelievable.

SURVIVAL RULES:

1. **Your wife may be a junkie.**
2. **Does she overdose on TV?**
3. **Does she get daily home delivery from her pharmacist?**
4. **Turn it to your advantage! Let her load up on soaps, TV mags, and diet pills and she'll leave you alone.**
5. **Enlist the aid of your local voodooist.**
6. **Act fast before she gets you first.**

Thirty-Four

WIVES BEHIND THE WHEEL

Wives have to drive, there's no getting around that, but do you have to ride with 'em? Not if you can help it, I say.

Is there anything more exasperating? Most of 'em drive like, well, old ladies, right? They're too slow or too fast or can't merge or back up properly. And can any of 'em turn a corner without bouncing the rear wheels off the curb?

Remember, though, not to be openly critical. Nothing pisses a woman off faster than to be told she can't drive as well as a man. Every woman thinks she's a female Richard Petty in spite of all the evidence to the contrary. To tell a woman she can't drive is to invite a rain of invectives down on your ass so don't do it.

The secret is to be subtle. Just deal with it as a reality and take whatever steps are necessary to preserve your sanity and physical well-being and keep your insurance rates down.

I knew a cop once who gave women driver's tests. The poor sap had ulcers the size of half-dollars and lived on a diet of Maalox and warm milk. Every new testee (if women can properly be called *testees*) was a new ambulatory nightmare. They'd drive over sidewalks and across lawns and make sudden left turns across the paths of oncoming semis and slam on the brakes in the middle of the block for no reason at all and sail blithely through red lights and then burst into tears when he flunked 'em.

And the ones who pass are little better. They just never seem to grasp the fundamentals of the thing. Turn signals mean you can turn at will once you've flicked it on for two flicks to warn others. Forty in the speed lane on a freeway is just safe driving. Doing your nails at traffic lights is reasonable behavior; after all, you *are* stopped, aren't you? And so on.

And what about parallel parking? No matter what claims the female sex makes to equality, they'll never ring quite true until women learn how to parallel park. I've seen women drivers ignore parking places that Ray Charles could back a semi into because they haven't mastered the trick. It just seems beyond them. Is it genetic? Cultural? Psychological? Who knows?

My own wife can't do it. If we go anywhere where parallel parking is a likelihood, I have to drive. There's just no way she can pull it off. She'll end up sticking four feet out into traffic or up on the sidewalk at some odd angle unknown to the science of geometry.

Maybe it's a question of hand-eye-foot coordination. Perhaps women can't work all three together in any kind of synchronized fashion. They pull up parallel to the car in front, look back and draw a bead on the parking space, and start turning too soon or too late and end by either overshooting it or cutting straight into the car parallel to 'em.

"HONEY, YOU KNOW THAT CONVERTIBLE
YOU ALWAYS WANTED?"

After six or seven tries, they finally give up and drive off looking for a spacious parking garage with head-in parking slots. Men know this, of course, and you'll often see some guy waiting patiently behind some broad who's vainly trying to squeeze a two-seater sports car into a Lincoln Town Car-sized space because he knows damn well she'll never make it and he can have the space himself.

So what can a man do about his wife's zany driving? That's easy, don't let her drive in your presence. When you go anywhere together, you always do the driving. Even on cross-country trips. It's a hassle, I know, but it's a lot less nerve-wracking in the long run.

It's also a good idea to make her drive the oldest car, the one with the four cylinder engine that does 0 to 60 in sixty seconds. What the hell, she's not going any place anyway. If she's going to back into mailboxes and sideswipe parked trees, at least let her bang up the '82 Chevette and not your brand-new sports coupe with the 32 valve engine and oversized cams, for God's sake. I mean, we're dealing with known quantities here and it makes sense to act accordingly.

If she bitches about this arrangement and demands her rights as an equal in today's modern society, tell her it's jake with you just as soon as she shows she can parallel park.

End of argument.

SURVIVAL RULES:

1. Don't ride with your wife.
2. Never let her try parallel parking.
3. Make her drive the oldest, slowest car.
4. Don't criticize, just do what's necessary.

Thirty-Five

HUSBAND AND WIFE LOOK-ALIKES

It's often said that people who stay married for a very long time actually begin to look like each other and assume a common personality. They even begin to *think* alike. Isn't that scary?

But is it true? It's easy to find out, just look at your friends and neighbors. If the wife is pear-shaped, does her old man look like a pear, too? If she's got three chins, how many has her husband? If she's gnome-like, has he turned into a gnome, too? Can they wear each others' clothes? Do their haircuts look alike?

One problem with researching this subject is the shortage of couples married long enough for these effects to have taken place. It seems the average marriage these days lasts about four years or so and you'd expect to see very few similarities developed over so short a time span.

Still, a quick study will show it is, in fact, true. If you're married long enough, you and your wife will slowly metamorphose into a single entity with almost indistinguishable characteristics. Something happens, maybe some odd kink in nature that craves a sort of multi-level synchronicity for some obscure reason, and people and things become one. Who knows?

What to do about it? Well, if you want to look like a rugged lumberjack type with terrific masculine features and broad shoulders when you're seventy-five, maybe you'd better marry a girl who looks like a lumberjack. Of course, that might not work if you look like the typical nerd because then your wife might turn out looking like you and the best your could hope for would be a nerdy lumberjack.

I guess the best thing is to marry a good-looker so at least you'll have a chance of being a handsome old-timer and be able to cut a wide swath through the widows and divorcees out there. Whatever you do, though, don't marry an ugly one, especially if you're no Mel Gibson yourself. Two ugly people can't help but merge into one even uglier and there's no sense giving yourself such a handicap if it can be avoided.

But there's a far more serious side to this business of looking alike, one that's a lot scarier than just looking like the old bat. I'm talking about the tendencies for couples to begin thinking alike. Can you imagine anything worse? I mean, if you start looking like your wife you can always grow a foot-long beard or wear dark glasses and a Groucho Marx moustache to hide the evidence, but what the hell are you supposed to do when the old crone takes over your damn mind, for Christ's sake?

Just think about it. If your wife's always been a fan of TV evangelists, you could spend your declining years watching the likes of Oral Robert and Jerry Fallwell — and liking it! Or end up addicted to soaps or game shows or Donahue, et al. What a horrible fate for a guy who's always prided himself on being a man of action, of vigor.

It starts simply enough. After x-years you'll notice occasions where you'll start a sentence and you wife'll say the exact same thing just as you say it. Or you'll think something and a moment later she'll say it aloud. Or you'll head out to the kitchen for some hot cocoa and she'll ask you to make her some. It's eerie.

The next thing you know you find out these psychic aberrations are happening routinely almost as though your minds were working as one. You feel yourself losing your sense of self and becoming something else, a new personality half you and half her.

Well, if it happens, it happens; after all, we can't fight nature, can we? Maybe not, but we can rig it in our favor. See, I've studied this phenomenon and I've noticed that one or the other tends to get the upper hand in these mental takeovers, and that the strongest mind tends to dominate the weaker one. Ergo, it behooves you to see that you're the one who does the dominating.

If you can dominate her mind, she could develop an interest in pool playing or TV football games or cigar smoking instead of forcing you into Jimmy Swaggert's camp and a life of TV soaps. It's all a question of who's got the most powerful mind.

Well, play mind games with the old bat. When she's not looking stare at the back of her head and think power thoughts. Say things in your head like, "I'm in charge. I command you to bend to my will. You have the weaker mind and I'm taking it over with my more powerful mind. You will change the channel to the football doubleheader *now!*" etc.

Or whisper similar things in her ear while she's sleeping. Use sleep-teaching techniques like playing tapes with recorded messages telling her she's a mental midget and must give herself over to a superior mind (i.e. yours).

Attack her mind when it's in its most defenseless state as, for instance, when she's watching General Hospital. Scientific studies show that women watching that show have minds operating with less power than a ten watt light bulb. Even your cat thinks on a higher plane, for Christ's sake. She'll be completely vulnerable then and easily dominated.

Fill the air with subliminal messages cleverly designed to influence her thinking without her being aware of it by interjecting whispered comments in the middle of normal conversations. Hint that she's coming unglued, forgetting things, losing her grip, slipping mentally. Hide her car keys on her and deride her failing memory when you have to find 'em for her.

Arrange it so she has to parallel park and then smile condescendingly and take over yourself when she's unable to do it. Show her in a lot of little ways that she's dealing with a mentality far superior to her own and she'll steadily surrender more and more to your proven superiority. Keep this up long enough and you're sure to end up in the mental driver's seat in your house and you'll have a chance to live out your own life at the end instead of living out hers.

Be careful, though. I knew one old duffer who followed this plan and it turned out his wily wife had already been employing the very same tactics against him for years before he even started. As a result his best efforts backfired and he became her alter ego and ended up singing in the church choir and ushering at Oral Roberts rallies.

It also happens, though, that his old lady was twice as smart as he was and the poor sap never had a chance in the mind-trip game. The obvious lesson is, of course, that you want to be careful not to marry a woman who's smarter than you are lest she dominate your weak-minded ass and turn you into a mental wimp and loser. Run ads for high school dropouts in the personals. Cruise fast-food restaurants. Look for bimbos with great bodies and low IQs until you find someone mentally inferior and marry her.

Avoid Phi Beta Kappas like the plague. Marry one of these types and she'll overpower your ass before you get back from the honeymoon. You'll end up a wishy-washy guy wearing aprons and horns and be despised by pool hall habitues throughout the city.

Yeah, I know, some of you guys will have a hard time finding wives dumber than you are but that's your problem. I can't work miracles, you know.

Who'd have thought it?

SURVIVAL RULES:

1. It's true, long-married couples tend to look alike.
2. Ergo, marry a pretty one.
3. What's worse, they tend to begin thinking alike.
4. Strong minds dominate weaker ones; so marry a weak-minded woman to insure your dominance.
5. As a precaution, marry one who likes beer, cigars, TV football, naked dancing girls, and trout fishing.
6. Hit her with power thoughts when her mind is a blank, (i.e. like when she's watching Dallas).

Thirty-Six

PREVAILING IN YOUR DIVORCE

Okay, so it's come down to this at last. You've done everything in your power to make your marriage a success and in spite of all that it's failed utterly and divorce is the only way out.

Don't lose sight of what's going on now. Remember that this woman is no longer an ally — if she ever was. She's a complete stranger, an enemy of the first magnitude, and dangerous in the extreme. Her sole purpose in life now is to do you as much harm as possible, to take everything you own and leave you devastated, broke, and bitter. Face it, you're dealing with evil incarnate, she's an opponent sans scruples, sans compassion, sans reason, sans fairness, sans even pity.

You see, in her mind the whole thing's your fault no matter what the circumstances. If she was a nag it was only because you refused to be reasonable and change your entire personality to suit her idea of what a husband should be. If she was a lousy housekeeper it was your fault because you never did your share of the work or always left your socks on the floor or whatever. If she was laying your bowling team it was only because you never showed her you cared by bringing her presents or flowers or diamond brooches.

The point is, she's the injured party and you're the screw-up and that's that. Know this and act accordingly. Expect nothing, prepare for anything.

Well, at least you should be a little smarter now than you were when you signed up for this cruise on the seas of matrimony. Where you went in blinded by love and unrealistic dreams of romance, you leave with clear vision enhanced by experience and reality of life in the real world.

Once divorce has been decided upon, the average guy will pack a suitcase and move out to an unheated room in a cheap hotel and leave his wife ensconced in the family homestead with all his worldly possessions.

Well, don't you do it.

No sir, that's always a mistake. If you're smart you'll make her move out. Suggest she go home to mother; it'll serve 'em both right and leave you in possession of your own possessions — a good position to be in when it comes to dividing property. Then have the locks changed to prevent her grasping mother from renting a truck and cleaning the place out in your absence.

If she refuses to leave, suggest that you both stay. You can move to the spare bedroom or sleep on the couch where you can keep an eye on things so she won't hold a garage sale and sell off your golf clubs and fishing stuff on you. Better yet, try to get her to go to the spare bedroom as it'll give you certain psychological advantages in the ensuing battle of wits and nerves.

If the old bat's absolutely intolerable for a single minute longer and she won't get out, then you'll have to go. But rent a truck first and haul away everything you value and store it where she can't get at it. Many an enraged wife has taken a pair of scissors to her husband's wardrobe and cut up his stock of eight hundred dollar suits or savaged his collection of custom-made fly rods just because she's pissed.

Okay, so you're in the cheap hotel and you've secured all your possessions, now get yourself a lawyer. Some guys think they can avoid expensive legal fees, especially if the wife cons 'em with the old let's-have-an-amicable-divorce scam. Beware a scene that unfolds like this.

"All right, then, let's be civil about this," she says cooly, assuming a sensible approach you've never seen before during your entire marriage. "There's no reason we can't get a divorce and still remain friends, is there?" she continues. "We can even save money on lawyers if we can just agree on a few things. I mean, why pay for two lawyers when we could get by with one?"

Does this argument sound familiar? Damn right, it's the very same scam you pulled on her when you set up that prenuptial agreement, remember? Only a sap would buy that — unless he's the one who proposes it and gets to use his own lawyer.

She may even try to dazzle you with sex in an effort to cloud your judgment in a propitious moment, so be on the alert for that. Of course, since you probably haven't seen her in anything resembling a sexy mode for quite some time, it may be hard to recognize it when you see it. But if you get the husky voice and meaningful look bit, it means she's up to no good so watch her ass. Don't forget, sex was never this girl's strong suit so why does she turn into a fireball now? Think, man, think.

An amicable divorce? Still friends? *There's no such thing, pal.* Hire the best legal gun you can find, preferably a specialist who's been divorced three or four times himself and knows the pitfalls from personal experience. Such a man will know the enemy for what she is and be less likely to be taken unawares with some newfangled ploy concocted by a wily foe.

Don't hire a woman lawyer. You can't trust 'em. Too many of 'em are feminists in disguise and dedicated to the proposition that all men are losers. Such a lawyer might subconsciously sympathize with the poor wife as a fellow sufferer who's being abused by a tyrannical man and load the dice in her favor. You could get stuck with higher support payments or fewer visitation rights or whatever.

But by all means encourage your wife to sign up a woman lawyer so your lawyer can intimidate her and overpower her with his manliness. Hope she gets one with a squeaky little voice and no presence at all. Or a sexpot with great boobs and short skirts and terrific gams, a woman everyone wants to lay but no one regards as a pro. Your lawyer and the judge can ogle her and wink at each other and do a little male bonding while teaming up to award you the lion's share of the swag.

You say that's an ugly scene, that it's degrading to women and beneath contempt? Of course it is, but remember you're locked in a fight to the death here, the winner gets the spoils and the loser nothing. This isn't amateur night or some kind of morality play, your future hangs in the balance and you've got to strike for the jugular, by God.

While the divorce is pending, it's a good idea to conduct yourself with some decorum so the old bat can't claim you're an unfit father or charge you with other heinous crimes which'll make you look bad in court. She'll probably have detectives on your ass at least some of the time so live circumspectly. You might even go to church, though, admittedly, that's pretty extreme. Or maybe you could work with orphans or lead a Boy Scout troop at least until the divorce is final.

Meanwhile, have your own detectives on her ass. If she's like most ex-wives, she's probably involved in some unsavory act somewhere and you need to know it. Maybe she's joined a motorcycle club and tattooed her boobs with an American eagle or something; if so, there isn't a judge anywhere who wouldn't cut her off without a dime and throw her ass out of his court as a disgrace to womanhood everywhere.

See how it works? It's dog against, well, bitch, in this case, and there are no rules except the ones the players make up as they go along.

If your wife earns more than you do, hold out for a settlement. Maybe there's some kind of community property law or something and you can take half of everything *she's* got. That'd be a twist, wouldn't it? If she earns a lot more than you do, it might be worth quitting your job and taking acting lessons or something. Tell 'em you're an out of work actor and your wife should support you in the style to which she's accustomed you or some such crap. Hey, it works for women all the time, doesn't it?

If there aren't any kids involved, and if you're not a millionaire, you'll probably just lose everything except your car and golf clubs. She'll get the rest. The house and furniture and stocks and bonds and summer cottage in Vermont and the rest will be awarded to her on the grounds that you're a man and deserve to be fleeced. Such thinking is a part of the fabric of the American judicial system. It's a holdover from the nineteenth century when women were helpless creatures and unable to fend for themselves in the world of work. Men were routinely stuck with grinding alimony payments that continued for life or until she remarried — and guess how often she was likely to do that? Judges everywhere still hold such views and you'll find it out when it's time to settle up.

If you're rich, she'll nail your ass for a fortune or know the reason why. Your only hope is you put together a really sound prenuptial agreement that'll hold water in court. Anything less and you'll think Jesse James and his gang moved through your bank account and stock portfolios in a raid to end all raids.

And if there are kids you'll also get it in the neck, and maybe you should. For one thing, the court automatically sides with the mother and kids and gives her everything along with child support because the kids need all the help they can get. Well, I say you should do the honorable thing and meet your responsibilities like a real man.

It's one thing to stave off the advances of a greedy bitch who's ugly and mean and grasping, but it's something else again to abandon kids you're personally responsible for. I say pay the support payments; what's more, I say pay more than the court-ordered amount to make sure your kids get a decent shake. Even though your ex-wife's a conniving bitch and you'd like to see her in hell, you can't send the kids along with her.

So it's over then. You married the girl of your dreams and she turned 'em into nightmares for you. You did the whole bit from dating to engagement to wedding to marriage and finally to divorce along with countless millions of other poor saps all over America. You've run the gamut, as they say, and now you're a better man for it.

Well, it wasn't a total loss, you know. Look at all the invaluable education and experience you've acquired. Sure, it cost you more than any sane man would voluntarily pay for a like experience, but you didn't have much choice once you'd crossed the bachelor's Rubicon by showing up at the church.

So you're a wiser man today, a survivor of one of life's most harrowing adventures and ready to move on to the next phase in your life, one that's bound to be better because you certainly won't make the same mistakes again.

Or will you?

SURVIVAL RULES:

1. Face it, divorce is almost inevitable.
2. Remember, there are no amicable divorces.
3. Get a top legal gun...
4. ...and drag out that prenuptial agreement!
5. Don't hire a woman lawyer, but encourage her to do so.
6. Try to have her use your lawyer, if possible.
7. Don't leave the house — make her go.
8. If you do leave, take all your stuff with you.
9. Demand a settlement if she makes more than you do.

Thirty-Seven

SINGLE AGAIN: NOW WHAT?

All right, the divorce is final. Your ex-wife's off on a cruise on your money and you're living on the edge of a slum while reorganizing your life. What now? Where do you go from here?

Well, for one thing, you enjoy your freedom. Hang around the pool hall until the place closes. Befriend guys with tattoos and earrings or Brooks Brothers suits depending on how you happen to feel and not on whether your wife'll approve or not. Never call home to let anybody know where the hell you are or when you're going to be home, by God! Be yourself for a change; it's a new experience and you'll find it exhilarating, even ennobling.

Enjoy it, I say, while you may, because if you're like all the rest — and you are, remember — you'll soon be involved with yet another little slip of a thing who seems to embody all things wonderful and is unique among women. She won't be any such thing, of course, and you really should know better by this time, but you won't.

Logically, you'd think the old adage once burned twice shy would apply to divorced guys, but it doesn't seem to work that way. Nobody ever learns, apparently. Ideally, you should avoid romantic entanglements for at least, say, six or eight years after a divorce. That's not to say you can't cut a wide swath through all the lovelies out there, but you should keep it light and not get involved beyond the occasional romp in the hay, as they say.

Keep 'em coming in bunches. Never date the same girl more than twice in a row because she'll start staking out territorial claims on your ass if you do. Most women regard a third date as an absolute binding commitment and begin composing engagement announcements and readying their hope chests.

Be sure all the players know about each other. Encourage lots of phone calls and leave your answering machine on when you have dates over. That way they'll hear the other babes leaving messages and know they don't have an inside track. If a woman gets pissed because you're going out with other girls, so what? Show her the door. Tell her, by God, she doesn't have any claims on your ass and you'll go out with whomever you please and you don't want to hear any more about it, either.

Leave other girls' stuff around your place to make the point even clearer. Have the odd earring on the coffee table, phone numbers lying about, panty hose behind the couch, two or three diaphragms of assorted sizes in the medicine cabinet, lipstick on everything in varying shades, and so on. You want all of 'em to know they're dealing with a free man who intends to stay that way, a guy in charge of his own destiny and not about to be conned into another marriage anytime soon.

Because you're being stalked, remember. These dames are vicious manhunters who'll stop at nothing. Fortunately, you're wise to 'em, aren't you?

Betty invites you over for a good home-cooked meal and what's your reaction? You're insulted, that's what. Does she think you're a damn amateur, for Christ's sake? Tell her to come up with something original and not insult you with dodges as old as civilization itself.

Sally wants you to meet her folks? Is she nuts?! Karen wants to give you an expensive gift? No way! Martha wants to keep a toothbrush in your bathroom in case she stays over? Over your dead body, by God! Only a fool would fall for anything so obvious and you're no fool, right?

Damn right. Now's the time to play the field, live it up a bit. If you can just stay single long enough, you should be able to regain some of your lost self and become a whole person again. In time you may even forget the whole unpleasant experience and finally emerge from the blue funk you were in all those years. And therein lies danger.

Once you've completely healed and the scars on your psyche have all but disappeared, you begin to believe in people again. You realize not every woman is a fiend from hell like your ex-wife. Some of 'em even seem nice. When you reach this point, you're vulnerable again and women can sense it. It brings out the blood lust in 'em, their pheromone output increases exponentially and their evil minds shift into high gear. Even their mothers are roused up by the excitement of the chase and they zero in on your ass like iron filings on a magnet.

The next thing you know you run into a particular woman who seems to have special charms, one who's different from all the others somehow. She has a special quality, there's something about her you can't quite put your finger on, and you're drawn in like a farmer into the bearded lady's tent at a carnival.

You take her out for that third date. She buys you a Rolex watch for your birthday — and you accept it. One day you open your medicine cabinet and there's an unfamiliar toothbrush inside. It's hers, of course. Before long you're having dinner with people she introduces as her parents and a sense of deja vu creeps over you and urges you to remember something you can't quite nail down.

You're a goner again, pal. The lady has vamped your ass good and it's too late. There's talk of engagements and rings and wedding rehearsals and showers and somehow it all seems vaguely familiar. At last you wake up one day and find all her stuff in your place. You wonder how there was room enough to hold all your junk and hers, too. And then you find she's sold off your golf clubs and softball stuff and the rest of your possessions and that's where all the room came from.

That's right, you're married again. And one day, probably not long after the honeymoon, you look across at your second wife as she natters on about how she wishes you wouldn't smoke cigars when her mother comes over, etc., and it comes to you in a rush.

Remember that special quality of hers, the one you couldn't quite put your finger on? Now you know what it was: She looks, acts, and sounds just like your first wife!

Incredible.

SURVIVAL RULES:

1. You're free at last, enjoy it.
2. Beware of new romantic entanglements.
3. Date widely and often.
4. Remember, after two dates they think they've got a commitment.
5. Be sure all of your dates know about the others so they won't get any crazy ideas.
6. Beware of home-cooked meals, her folks, toothbrushes in your medicine cabinet, expensive gifts, etc.
7. Remember, she only seems different.
8. Don't panic when you realize you've married an exact copy of your first wife. Everybody does it.

Thirty-Eight

THE SUMMING UP

So what have we learned? Well, let's take a look and see. Let's begin with the dating years and work up — or down, depending on how you look at it. Start by remembering women are basically all alike and all want the same things, and that these things are all in absolute conflict with the things you want. Ergo, choose one for those qualities which are most likely to benefit you directly. In other words, marry money if you can.

Also, marry a pretty girl as it's just as easy to fall in love with a pretty girl as it is an ugly one. Have a long engagement; six years seems about right. Remember to establish bowling night and Friday poker games and fight to keep 'em. And let her know you'll handle the money right from the start so it'll never be an issue later on.

Once you've tied the knot, the war begins in earnest. Go along with any wedding plans she and her mother come up with for the sake of harmony, but don't pay for any of 'em. The bride's family pays dowries, remember? It's an age-old custom all over the world and we revere custom, don't we? You bet your ass we do.

Be on the offensive, especially during the first few weeks and months of your marriage. Patterns established early on will be almost impossible to change later so make damn sure the ones that get fixed in your house are ones you can live with for the next fifty or so years. It's all a matter of planning ahead.

Keep an eye on your mother-in-law. The old bat'll hurt you if she can. If possible, move to another state where she can't find you. If all else fails, ban her ass from your house and refuse to accept incoming calls.

Unless your wife is an heiress, put her to work. And make sure she's got productive skills when you marry her so she can get a good job and bring some ready cash into the house. Don't let her gamble or develop expensive habits such as buying a lot of clothes or jewelry.

Divide the housework as God intended it to be divided — say something like ninety percent for her and ten for you since that seems to be a reasonable division. Refer her to the Old Testament if she complains. Remember, you never heard about Moses or Job or any of that bunch doing the damn dishes or scrubbing floors.

Don't forget her mother is only an older model of her daughter so if the old bat's overweight and ugly and has the personality of a demon from hell, her daughter will be a carbon copy twenty years later. Watch her weight. Don't let her get fat on you. Refuse to listen to talk about slow metabolism or bad genes or any of that other crap she'll come up with as an excuse for turning into the Pillsbury dough girl. Guys with fat wives have only themselves to blame.

Let her spend money on makeup and beauty shops. She can hide a lot of ugly under a good paint job and look better when you take her out in public.

Don't let her put horns on you. Keep a wary eye on all repairmen, wavy-haired neighbors, slim Italians in tight pants, et al. Your honor's at stake and you mustn't drop your guard for a minute or you'll end up an object of derision amongst your peers.

Have an occasional affair yourself as it's not only natural for men but actually right for 'em to do so. But be discreet, show some respect for her feelings and don't bring women home while she's there. If she complains, cite the Bible again and point out all the concubines those old-timers had back then.

Don't let her watch TV movies about wives bumping husbands off and retiring to the Riviera on the poor bastard's insurance money.

Agree to counseling when the time comes — and it will! — but rig it against her. Hire Tony.

When divorce is imminent, move fast and first. Seize everything and hide it. Clean out safe deposit boxes and joint accounts before she beats you to 'em. Hire a good lawyer. Hit her ass with that prenuptial agreement you had the foresight to set up. No man escapes from a divorce with a whole skin, but you just may get away with half a skin if you're ruthless, cunning, and devious enough.

Be wary after the divorce. Only a sap hurries from one marriage to another without giving himself some time to enjoy the fruits of his well-earned freedom.

Value the experience. Getting married and going through all the crap and getting divorced is the thing to do. It's part of our culture, a way of life. Everybody does it. Most of us manage to survive it and some even profit from the whole thing.

I might add that there's a slim chance you'll be one of the lucky ones and end up with a wife you can not only live with but actually like.

Oh, it's a slim chance, all right, but it does happen. I know because it happened to me.

Astonishing.

TITLES BY CCC PUBLICATIONS

—NEW BOOKS—

FOR **MEN** ONLY (How To Survive Marriage)

HORMONES FROM HELL (The Ultimate *Women's* Humor Book)

GIFTING RIGHT (How To Give A Great Gift Every Time! For Any Occasion! And On Any Budget!)

THE SUPERIOR PERSON'S GUIDE TO EVERYDAY IRRITATIONS

HOW TO TALK YOUR WAY OUT OF A TRAFFIC TICKET

YOUR GUIDE TO CORPORATE SURVIVAL

WHAT DO WE DO NOW?? (The Complete Guide For All New Parents Or Parents-To-Be)

—SPRING 1991 RELEASES—

THE Unofficial WOMEN'S DIVORCE MANUAL

HUSBANDS FROM HELL

HOW TO REALLY PARTY!!!

THE GUILT BAG [Accessory Item]

—BEST SELLERS—

NO HANG-UPS (Funny Answering Machine Messages)

NO HANG-UPS II

NO HANG-UPS III

GETTING EVEN WITH THE ANSWERING MACHINE

HOW TO GET EVEN WITH YOUR EXes

HOW TO SUCCEED IN SINGLES BARS

TOTALLY OUTRAGEOUS BUMPER-SNICKERS

THE "MAGIC BOOKMARK" BOOK COVER [Accessory Item]

—CASSETTES—

NO HANG-UPS TAPES (Funny, Pre-recorded Answering Machine Messages With Hilarious *Sound Effects*) — In Male or Female Voices

Vol. I: GENERAL MESSAGES

Vol. II: BUSINESS MESSAGES

Vol. III: 'R' RATED

Vol. IV: SOUND EFFECTS ONLY

Vol. V: CELEBRI-TEASE (Celebrity Impersonations)

Coming Soon:

Vol. VI: MESSAGES FOR SPORTS FANS